HUMAN RIGHTS, SERIOUS CRIME AND CRIMINAL PROCEDURE

by

ANDREW ASHWORTH Q.C.
Vinerian Professor of English Law
All Souls College, Oxford

Published under the auspices of
THE HAMLYN TRUST

LONDON
SWEET & MAXWELL
2002

Published in 2002 by Sweet & Maxwell Limited of
100 Avenue Road, Swiss Cottage,
London NW3 3PF
Typeset by LBJ Typesetting Ltd of Kingsclere
Printed in England by
MPG Books Ltd, Bodmin, Cornwall

No natural forests were destroyed to make this product;
only farmed timber was used and replanted

**A CIP catalogue record for this book is available from the British
Library**

ISBN 0421 782900 (HB)
0421 783001 (PB)

Andrew Ashworth Q.C.
2002

ONE WEEK LOAN

AUSTRALIA
Law Book Co.
Sydney

CANADA and USA
Carswell
Toronto

HONG KONG
Sweet & Maxwell Asia

NEW ZEALAND
Brookers
Wellington

SINGAPORE and MALAYSIA
Sweet & Maxwell Asia
Singapore and Kuala Lumpur

ACKNOWLEDGEMENTS

I am grateful to the Hamlyn trustees for inviting me to give the 2001 lectures, and for their kindness and efficiency in making arrangements for the three lectures to be delivered. The first lecture was given at De Montfort University, and I am grateful to Professor Richard Card for his sympathetic chairing. The second lecture was delivered at the Queen's University, Belfast: Professor Norma Dawson was most generous with her time and ensured that my visit went smoothly, and I am grateful to Professor Stephen Livingstone for agreeing at short notice to act as chair. The third lecture was given at Cardiff University, where Professor Andrew Grubb was a sensitive chair and a welcoming host. The chairman of the Hamlyn trustees, Professor Barry Rider, took the trouble to attend all three lectures, and maintained unobtrusive oversight of all the arrangements. I am glad to have this opportunity of recording my deep gratitude to him.

In preparing the lectures I was able to take advantage of research assistance from a number of Oxford students, Prince Saprai being particularly helpful. In finalising the text of the lectures, I have had the benefit of comments and suggestions from a number of people. Several of those who attended the lectures either spoke to me at the time or wrote to me subsequently, and I am grateful to them all. Special thanks go to Colm Campbell, Caroline Fennell, Liora Lazarus, Mike Redmayne, Adam Tomkins and Andrew von Hirsch for reading and commenting on drafts. And it is a great pleasure to be able to thank my partner Von for her support throughout the preparation, writing and delivery of the lectures.

Andrew Ashworth
Oxford
February 2002

TABLE OF CONTENTS

THE HAMLYN LECTURES

The Hamlyn Lectures

THE HAMLYN TRUST

The Hamlyn Trust owes its existence to the will of the late Miss Emma Warburton Hamlyn of Torquay, who died in 1941 at the age of 80. She came of an old and well-known Devon family. Her father, William Bussell Hamlyn, practised in Torquay as a solicitor and J.P. for many years, and it seems likely that Miss Hamlyn founded the trust in his memory. Emma Hamlyn was a woman of strong character, intelligent and cultured, well-versed in literature, music and art, and a lover of her country. She travelled extensively in Europe and Egypt, and apparently took considerable interest in the law and ethnology of the countries and cultures that she visited. An account of Miss Hamlyn by Dr Chantal Stebbings of the University of Exeter may be found, under the title "The Hamlyn Legacy", in volume 42 of the published lectures.

Miss Hamlyn bequeathed the residue of her estate on trust in terms which it seems were her own. The wording was thought to be vague, and the will was taken to the Chancery Division of the High Court, which in November 1948 approved a Scheme for the administration of the trust. Paragraph 3 of the Scheme, which closely follows Miss Hamlyn's own wording, is as follows:

> "The object of the charity is the furtherance by lectures or otherwise among the Common People of the United Kingdom of Great Britain and Northern Ireland of the knowledge of the Comparative Jurisprudence and Ethnology of the Chief European countries including the United Kingdom, and the circumstances of the growth of such jurisprudence to the Intent that the Common People of the United Kingdom may realise the privileges which in law and custom they enjoy in comparison with other European Peoples and realising and appreciating such privileges may recognise the responsibilities and obligations attaching to them."

The Trustees are to include the Vice-Chancellor of the University of Exeter, representatives of the Universities of London, Leeds, Glasgow, Belfast and Wales and persons co-opted. At present there are eight Trustees:

From the outset it was decided that the objects of the Trust could best be achieved by means of an annual course of public lectures of outstanding interest and quality by eminent Lecturers, and by their subsequent publication and distribution to a wider audience. The first of the Lectures were delivered by the Rt Hon. Lord Justice Denning (as he then was) in 1949. Since then there has been an unbroken series of annual Lectures. A complete list of the Lectures may be found on pages ix to xii. The Trustees have also, from time to time, provided financial support for a variety of projects which, in various ways, have disseminated knowledge or have promoted a wider public understanding of the law.

The 53rd series of lectures was delivered by Professor Andrew Ashworth, at De Montfort University, Queen's University, Belfast, and Cardiff Law School, during November 2001. The Board of Trustees would like to record its appreciation to Professor Ashworth and also to the three University law schools, which generously hosted these lectures.

April 2002   **BARRY A.K. RIDER**
                                                  Chairman of the Trustees

TABLE OF CASES

Table of Cases

Table of Cases

Table of Cases

Table of Cases

1. Why bother with Rights when Public Safety is at risk?

A. INTRODUCTION

(i) Theme of the lectures

These lectures tackle a problem which has social, political and legal dimensions. It is at once a practical problem, a problem of policy, and also a problem of deep principle. It arises in this way. The United Kingdom, along with all other members of the Council of Europe, signed and ratified the European Convention on Human Rights some 50 years ago. The United Kingdom has recently gone further: the Human Rights Act 1998 requires British courts and other public authorities to act in accordance with rights under the Convention. Yet those two developments run parallel to growing demands for greater powers to tackle serious crime. Over the last 50 years[1] military language has increasingly been used to emphasise the urgency of the situation—the war on drugs, the fight against organised crime, the anti-terrorist offensive, and so forth. In the last decade there has been a distinct repressive turn in the politics of criminal justice in this country, manifested in such policies as the restrictions on the right of silence introduced in 1994, the mandatory minimum prison sentences introduced in 1997, and harsher sentencing which has led to an increase in the prison population of over 50 per cent in five years.[2] The lectures examine the clash between these two sets of ideologies, the promotion of human rights and the struggle against serious crime. Can both ideologies be pursued simultaneously without compromise? If there is to be compromise, how should it be arranged? Should the rights of suspects and defendants be diminished, or should the struggle against serious crime be curtailed? On what basis, and by whom, should such decisions be taken? And if there is to be any diminution of human rights, does that mean that they are not really human rights at all? These and other questions will run through the lectures.

The enactment of the Human Rights Act in 1998 was the subject of great professional debate and some public discussion, but there was very little mention of the substance of many of the rights that were then being "incorporated" into British law. No doubt everyone is in favour of the right to a fair trial, but did people really know what that right has been taken to mean under the Convention? I think it is startling that some of the key rights received very little discussion,[3] and indeed that there was probably a fair amount of ignorance both amongst lawyers and in government circles of what the contours of these rights are. The chief aim of this first lecture is to provoke some wider discussion about some of the central "fair trial" rights, beginning with brief discussions of the idea of human rights, of the value of accurate adjudication, and of process values and legitimacy. This leads into part D, where some arguments for and against 10 aspects of procedural fairness are aired. The final part reviews some of the issues of public safety which form a central plank of the justification for the criminal justice system. At an early stage of preparing these lectures it was decided not to focus on anti-terrorist measures but rather to focus on responses to other forms of serious crime, particularly drug trafficking, organized crime and serious fraud. Although the official reaction to the events of September 11, 2001 has again raised deep questions about the commitment of governments to human rights, the focus of the lectures remains unchanged. There will be some references to anti-terrorist measures in all three lectures, and we should remain aware of the danger that "extraordinary" powers which are supported as necessary for "the fight against terrorism" may come to be normalised by being applied progressively to other forms of serious crime.[4]

(ii) The idea of human rights

While a substantial part of what follows is concerned with human rights, I should state at the outset that I do not approach the lectures on the basis that either human rights in general or the rights under the European Convention on Human Rights are unqualified goods. I am not one of those who "treat human rights as an object of devotion rather than calculation"[5]— although, as will be evident, I assign greater importance to them than many do. I recognise that both elements of the term, "human" and "rights", are open to debate; I recognise that what are called human rights are relevant only to some of the issues of criminal procedure that concern me; and I also recognise that in practice so much depends on the interpretation of the human rights texts and their application "on the ground" rather than on the often broad and over-ambitious terms in which they are drafted and promoted. The lectures employ the term "human rights" for convenience, that convenience arising from the fact that the focus will chiefly be on the rights guaranteed by Article 6 of the European Convention. So far as I am concerned, however, the adjective "human" could be replaced by another adjective such as "fundamental", "basic" or even "constitutional"—indeed, it is worth recalling that the Convention's full title is the European Convention for the Protection of Human Rights and Fundamental Freedoms. The purpose of these adjectives is to signify the special respect in which these rights, rather than others, should be held, and the special weight they should be assigned in decision-making about general policies or individual cases.

In view of the powerful symbolism often attaching to the term "human rights", two more points must be made at this early stage. First, the focus of these lectures lies some distance from the realm in which the rhetorical force of the concept of human rights is at its greatest. Atrocities taking place in Bosnia, Rwanda and elsewhere are characterised as violations of human rights, and much of the outrage at such events and the sympathy for the victims and their families comes to be associated with the notion of human rights violations. Such events could be described and condemned without reference to human rights, but it may be thought that recognition of the events as violations of human rights lends a further layer of objectivity to the condemnation. It is not clear whether that added objectivity is commonly associated with human rights in the relatively narrow field with which these lectures are concerned—rights in criminal procedure, deriving from the rule-of-law safeguards set out in Articles 5, 6 and 7 of the European Convention. Here the focus is changed, because these rights attach to those suspected or convicted of crimes, and there is likely to be far less sympathy for such people in general.[6] Occasionally there is publicity about British people held abroad without charge and without access to family, legal advice or even embassy officials; but, certainly so far as the most prominent mass media in this country are concerned, the idea of human rights is associated much more with grave atrocities, or even with rights such as the freedom of expression and privacy, than with the rights of suspects and defendants.

The second preliminary point is that human rights are properly seen as minimum guarantees and safeguards, and not as a manifesto for a just society. Respect for human rights may be seen as a necessary condition of a just society, but it would hardly be sufficient—many other social and economic reforms would be necessary in order to secure the kind of social justice that many would regard as acceptable, let alone ideal. Thus no assumption is made here that to discuss rights is to deal with the most important social issues. Moreover, we must be on our guard about human rights talk that vaunts general principles without ensuring that in practice the proclaimed rights are respected—which often requires the investment of public money, and changes of attitude and ethical orientation among those officials who have day-to-day interaction with rights-bearers. Put in straightforward language, this means that the police and other law enforcement agencies must respect human rights in their work, before there can be any rejoicing in the high-sounding declarations of human rights.

(iii) Criminal procedure and human rights

The very concept of criminal procedure is often viewed with suspicion, insofar as it is taken to imply technicalities which may turn into obstacles. The United Kingdom has brought the substance of the European Convention on Human Rights into its legal systems, but there have been murmurings among some Ministers of the Crown and some judges about the kinds of rights declared in the Convention. Whatever the "spirit of the Convention" means in Strasbourg, there is evidence in some government and judicial circles of a spirit of minimalism, particularly when it comes to the rights of suspects and defendants in the criminal process. The unspoken attitude of some seems to be that, if we have to have the Convention, we should confine its influence as narrowly as possible. Yet this attitude co-exists with declarations of great enthusiasm for the Human Rights Act and the Convention.

Thus Lord Bingham was one of the judges who had argued the case for incorporating the Convention into domestic law. In his 1993 article he wrote strongly about the importance of having the Convention available to British courts as a kind of "higher law", agreeing that "the protection of its citizens' fundamental rights is generally seen as an important function of civil society."[7] Yet his approach to the first major decision on the Human Rights Act 1998, *Brown v. Stott*,[8] consists of a search for ways of minimising the effect of Article 6 and its jurisprudence. Similarly, it was the then Home Secretary, Jack Straw, who presented the Human Rights Bill to Parliament with high commendations and an apparent pride in his role in what he saw as a historic measure: "In future years historians may regard the Bill as one of the most important measures of this Parliament."[9] Again, "the Human Rights Act 1998 is the most significant statement of human rights in domestic law since the 1689 Bill of Rights."[10] As Mr Straw explained more fully in the House of Commons:

> Nothing in the Bill will take away the freedoms that our citizens already enjoy. However, those freedoms alone are not enough: they need to be complemented by positive rights that individuals can assert when they believe that they have been treated unfairly by the state, or that the state and its institutions have failed properly to protect them. The Bill will guarantee to everyone the means to enforce a set of basic civil and political rights, establishing a floor below which standards will not be allowed to fall.[11]

However, there were soon doubts about how low the floor really was. The same Mr Straw presented to the House the Dangerous People with Severe Personality Disorder Bill 2000 and the bills which became the Terrorism Act 2000, the Regulation of Investigatory Powers Act 2000, and the Criminal Justice and Police Act 2001—all of which display the kind of minimalism described above, in the form of a government determination to provide for individual suspects or defendants the most slender safeguards for which there was a possible argument of Convention compatibility.

In so far as this minimalist attitude is to be found—and I believe it may be stronger in the area of criminal justice than in some other spheres—it tends to undermine the rights which are declared by the Convention to be fundamental freedoms. This prompts questions about why we should honour these rights at all. Do the rights in the European Convention, and particularly those in Article 6 as interpreted by the European Court of Human Rights, have any intrinsic claim on our attention? Should we be enthusiastic about them, treating them as fundamental rights on which we ought to be prepared to build, or should we regard them merely as inconvenient obstacles to be avoided when public policy is being developed?

(iv) A hypothetical case

I want to start this first lecture with a hypothetical case. Let us suppose it is an autumn evening. You have to go out to a meeting. You have a son or a brother aged about 18, and you leave him at home with another young man of the same age who is visiting him. You arrive back home at 9 p.m. to find a police car nearby. On enquiring what has happened, you are told that a burglary has been reported at a house a short distance away; that two young men were seen in the street adjacent to the house; that they had evidently been drinking; and that they were asked to go to the police station for questioning and declined, so they were arrested on suspicion of burglary and taken to the police station. It transpires that one is your son (or brother), and the other is the young man who was visiting him. How would you wish them to be treated by the police? Should it be for the police to decide how long and under what conditions they are kept, or should they have rights? This example might usefully be borne in mind, and used as a kind of thought experiment, as we consider the case for procedural rights, particularly in part D below.

B. THE VALUE OF ACCURATE ADJUDICATION

The first thing to acknowledge is that we are dealing here with a potentially serious crime, burglary. We all have an interest in the prevention of such crimes, and in the thorough investigation of those crimes when they happen, with a view to the prosecution, conviction and sentencing of offenders. This is not just a matter of public interest, for which we expect the government to make adequate provision. It is also in the interests of every citizen as a potential victim. So, as we go on to think about the rights of suspected and accused persons, we must bear in mind the social importance of tackling crime.

At the same time, we must consider the position of a person suspected of burglary or a similar crime. Where we, or our friends or family are concerned, this brings home to us the basic expectation of fair dealing at the hands of officials. There is a considerable power differential between the police and the individual suspect; moreover, the power that the police and other law enforcement agencies have is supposedly exercised in the public interest, which should mean that it is exercised within defined limits and is subject to procedures of accountability. From the individual suspect's point of view, the expectation of fair dealing is great when there is much at stake. Thus a criminal conviction may involve a stain on one's record, and will usually involve some kind of punishment—a deprivation of money, restrictions on one's liberty, and even the risk of losing one's liberty. Where there is a criminal investigation, as in my example, there is so much at stake—in our hypothetical case, temporary deprivation of liberty—that citizens ought to be able to insist on guarantees of a fair procedure.

Immediately I begin to go down this track, I will rightly be stopped by the sceptic, who will say:

> surely the whole purpose of the criminal process is to produce accurate outcomes, that is, to convict the guilty and to acquit the innocent? Fairness has two sides to it. There may be inaccurate outcomes in either direction. Yes, it is very unfair to an individual to be wrongly convicted. But isn't it equally unfair to the public at large if a guilty person is acquitted?

This is an important challenge. To start discussing fairness without taking account of these points would be wrong. So let us give some consideration to the ideal of accuracy—that criminal procedure should, above all, be designed to ensure the maximum accuracy of outcomes. Is this a defensible view?

(i) Accuracy as the primary objective

It seems axiomatic that the achievement of accurate outcomes should be the primary aim of criminal procedure and the laws of evidence. In principle, the ideal system would be one that convicts the guilty only and acquits the innocent only. There is, however, considerable divergence of opinion on the best way of achieving this goal. Jeremy Bentham, who recognised accuracy (his term was "rectitude") as the primary objective of criminal procedure in his writings some two centuries ago,[12] was critical of technical systems of proof. English law, which, in the modern day as well as in Bentham's time, contains many rules restricting the kinds of evidence admissible in court, was a target for his criticisms. His preferred approach was to allow all evidence to be given except the irrelevant or superfluous, although his secondary concern was the avoidance of undue delay and expense, and he recognised that compromises would need to be made on this score. In his system, rectitude would be assisted by providing sanctions against perjury.

(ii) Tribunals and their fallibilities

What can be the objections to such a straightforward system? Four principal kinds of objection will be mentioned here and developed throughout this chapter. The first is that to adopt Bentham's view may not be to ensure accuracy in all methods of trial. The English system, with its reliance on juries and on lay magistrates, contains a number of restrictions on the admissibility of evidence which tend to be justified by the probable prejudicial effect on lay minds of hearing certain kinds of evidence. For example, the general rule that a defendant's previous convictions may not be used in evidence against him is often defended by saying that lay minds would too readily jump to the conclusion that the existence of a criminal record makes it more likely that the defendant committed the crime charged. This is not the place to test whether the factual basis for that justification is sustainable;[13] what we must surely accept is that the goal of maximum accuracy must be responsive to different systems of trial and procedure. Of course this does not mean that rules of evidence and procedure must be shaped in a certain way: one could just as well argue that it is our method of trial, rather than the rules of criminal procedure, that ought to be altered in order to deliver greater accuracy of outcomes.[14] Yet under the current English system, if accuracy is to be the primary goal, it may be justifiable to exclude or restrict certain types of evidence if the lay tribunal seems likely to misinterpret them.[15]

(iii) "Guilt" and its fallibilities

A second and related objection is that rectitude (or accuracy) may not be the solid, objective concept that some believe it to be. It is not uncommon to hear reference to someone being "caught red-handed" or being "factually guilty" when they are known to have done a certain act[16]; but this may not be accurate if they have a possible defence to the crime, or if the prosecution is unable to prove the intent or dishonesty needed to secure a conviction. Identification evidence is notoriously fallible, even where the witness is sure about it. False confessions are a well-documented phenomenon,[17] however difficult it may be for many of us to imagine circumstances in which we might confess to a crime we did not commit. There is a whole array of reasons for taking a critical view of so-called "expert evidence," scrutinising both the reliability of forensic science procedures and the interpretation of results and events.[18] These doubts undermine the very notion of "factual guilt", and contradict the assumption that it is a reliable or "objective" concept. The doubts suggest that the idea of a system of "free proof", even as an ideal, must be approached with caution.

(iv) The effects of power differentials

A third line of objection to Bentham's approach is that it takes no account of the differences in power and resources between the State (in the form of police and prosecution) and the defence. In most situations it is the police who hold the practical power over the suspect,[19] and without an array of procedural protections there is the danger that law enforcement agencies might take advantage of the weak position of suspects at a time that is crucial to the construction of the case. Not all suspects exercise their right to have a lawyer present; even if that right is exercised, there are always times at which there may be interaction between police and suspect without a lawyer being present; and even if a lawyer is present, he or she may have insufficient information on which to base sound advice, or may fail to protect the client against unfair tactics. The result may be unfair practices or unreliable evidence which might detract from the overall goal of maximum accuracy.

(v) Constraints on the pursuit of accuracy

A fourth objection is that Bentham's system assigns no significance at all to fairness considerations, for example, whether evidence obtained in certain ways should be excluded from a trial, or whether it is fair to draw adverse inferences from a suspect's refusal to answer questions. Since much of the discussion in the remainder of the chapter is on this theme, I will say little more at this stage. But Bentham's view was strong: rectitude or accuracy should not give way to alleged considerations of fairness, except in the extreme case of communications between priest and penitent, where he recognised that the priest should not be compelled to testify to what was said.

C. PROCESS VALUES AND LEGITIMACY

This last objection to Bentham's view casts the spotlight back on the idea of fairness. What is the kernel of this idea, and are there good reasons for insisting on it? The answer to this question is the main focus of the remaining parts of this lecture. For the present it is appropriate to consider what other values one might expect criminal procedure to serve, besides maximum accuracy of outcomes. The claims of four other values—public participation; communication; upholding victims' rights; and upholding basic protections for defendants—may be considered briefly.

(i) Public participation

The value of public participation lies in ensuring that criminal justice is not administered purely by lawyers or officials, that it is administered in public and in an open way, and (perhaps) by serving as one form of check on the power of officials. Justifications of these kinds are put forward in favour of preserving the use of juries in (some) criminal trials, and of preserving the lay magistracy. Much more could be written about participation, the value of which is clearly linked to concepts of citizenship and community. It resonates particularly with much contemporary thought on communitarian themes and on restorative justice, but its significance is dependent on neither. It can be seen as a value wherever social co-operation is required.

(ii) Communication

The value of communication has two separate aspects. One is communication with the public or the community: procedures should be transparent and communicative in their nature, in the sense that it should be plain to people what their purpose and effect is. This is an instrumental value, inasmuch as it contributes to the transparency of the processes. A separate value is communication directly with the defendant, in the sense of treating him or her as a citizen worthy of respect as a thinking member of the social community. This means that it should be clear what the purposes of all the procedural steps are, and their application in the particular case should be explicable and justifiable in a way that respects him or her as an autonomous person. In many criminal justice systems these are pious hopes, because the system is dominated by professionals (police, lawyers) whose methods of working often do not involve patient explanations of each procedural step. Yet this is not to doubt the value of communication; rather, it casts doubt on whether we achieve it in our system, or whether we even count it as an objective.

(iii) Upholding victims' rights

The third set of values raises issues which go well beyond the scope of these lectures. Much is heard about the importance of fairness for defendants when insisting that criminal justice systems respect fundamental values, but rather less has been heard until recent years about fairness to victims. This provokes the question: what are the procedural rights of victims? So far as the European Convention on Human Rights is concerned, no procedural rights for victims find a place in either the 1950 Declaration or any of the subsequent Protocols, although victims have the same rights as other citizens, such as the right to security of person (Article 5) and the right to respect for their private life (Article 8), which may be relevant during criminal investigations and trials.[20] But the present enquiry should not be limited by the boundaries of the Convention, and so the questions of victims' rights should still be discussed.

Victims should receive personal support in coping with the aftermath of the offence, information about available help and about the progress of the case, and so forth,[21] but whether they should have the right to be consulted at certain key stages of decision-making (such as charge, remand, plea negotiation, sentence, release from custody) depends on the nature of their interest in criminal proceedings. My argument, developed extensively elsewhere,[22] is that the criminal process and sentencing are procedures to be carried out in the public interest (in which the interests of the victim count for no more than that of any other citizen), with decisions taken by impartial and independent tribunals and not in a forum in which a victim, who is unlikely to be either independent or impartial, has a voice. There are exceptions to this: compensation is clearly a matter on which the victim should have a voice, and the victim's perspective is relevant to decisions on remand or release from custody in the sense that considerations of public protection often become concerns about the protection of victims. The general position, however, is that it would be the antithesis of fairness if defendants' treatment were to be influenced by whether the particular victim was vengeful or forgiving or neither. Beyond procedural rights, victims should have the same rights as any other citizen under the Articles of the Convention.

(iv) Upholding basic protections for defendants

Fourthly, we come to the upholding of basic safeguards for defendants. Many countries have a written constitution which includes a number of fundamental rights for suspects and defendants in the criminal process: such constitutions are seen, for example, in Germany and in Ireland and in many countries of the British Commonwealth, including most of those which still send their final appeals to the Privy Council in London. The United Kingdom has no such constitutional guarantees, but it does now have the Human Rights Act 1998, which gives a certain legal force and recognition to most of the core rights of the European Convention. If a legal system proclaims rights in this way, it follows that its criminal procedure should be shaped so as to avoid conflicts with the various rights set out in such a fundamental document. In this way it can claim to fulfil a central requirement of a *Rechtsstaat*; and adherence to rule-of-law values of this kind seems likely to enhance citizens' acceptance of the fairness and legitimacy of the processes.[23]

(v) Conflicting values

As soon as we recognise that there may be two or more of these highly-respected values, we need to face the problem that they will inevitably conflict in their application to the criminal justice system. If one is thinking about an ideal criminal justice system, it is insufficient to say that the goals of that system are accuracy, fairness, participation and communication: that may sound good, but it fails to indicate how conflicts are resolved, and how the goals are to be prioritised. For example, there will be some occasions on which respect for fair procedures may mean that we do not maximise the chances of an accurate outcome. Consider also the primary aim of the Home Office:

> To work with individuals and communities to build a safe, just and tolerant society enhancing opportunities for all and in which rights and responsibilities go hand in hand, and the protection and security of the public are maintained and enhanced.[24]

This high-sounding objective is riven with conflicts, and there is no mention of how they might be resolved. What appears as a splendid aim against which no-one could possibly argue—"to build a safe, just and tolerant society"—glosses over the inevitable conflicts between the kinds of policy that would conduce to improved public safety, to greater justice, and to broader tolerance.

Let us conclude this section by briefly considering what must be the starkest conflict between accuracy and rights, the one which occurs where the question is whether to use torture to obtain evidence. A person's right not to be tortured is regarded as fundamental by all human rights documents. There may be a strong temptation to authorise its use when a few individuals appear to hold information on which the lives of many people may depend, as suggested in the United States following the events of September 11, 2001.[25] However, human rights documents hold that, no matter how effective torture may be in extracting the truth, it is a method which ought never to be used. Many would add that, if torture has been used, a court should refuse to receive a confession obtained thereby, because it would taint the legitimacy of the whole proceedings. Issues of this kind will be discussed further below. For the moment, I merely want to show that the values we respect may come into conflict with one another, and that those conflicts need to be resolved. Simply to articulate a number of values that criminal procedures ought to respect and promote is the beginning of a lengthy discussion, not the end.

D. EXPLORING PROCEDURAL FAIRNESS

I began this lecture by describing the arrest of two young men on suspicion of burglary, and asked what rights one might expect them to have. The seriousness of the crime itself was recognised, but of course that cuts in different ways—the crime is serious in general social terms, it may be serious for the victim, and its seriousness is a significant factor for the suspect. In this section I will sketch the rationales for 10 possible procedural rights for persons accused of potentially serious crimes. The purpose is to generate wider discussion on the content and scope of rights which we have not only accepted as fundamental but also brought into the domestic laws of this country. All but one of them are rights recognised by the European Convention on Human Rights—rights with a national and international pedigree. However, it would be wrong to assume that the list of European Convention rights is, or ought to be, fixed for all time, and therefore we should have an eye to possible developments of rights. For that reason I include among the ten rights one which has no settled national or international pedigree at this stage: it will at least serve to demonstrate the need to think further about existing categories of rights. The ten rights are:

1. the right to be presumed innocent

2. the privilege against self-incrimination

3. the right of silence

4. the right to legal aid and assistance

5. the right to be brought promptly before a court

6. the right to release pending trial

7. the right to disclosure of documents

8. the right to confront witnesses

9. the right to be tried on evidence not obtained by violation of fundamental rights

10. the right not to be placed in double jeopardy.

The discussion of each possible right will necessarily be brief, because the purpose is to examine the general contours of arguments for procedural fairness. In respect of each right there will also be a sceptic's challenge: why should we not reject this right? The views of cynics and sceptics are important if a healthy discussion of fundamentals is to be generated: no matter how high the authority for certain rights, their claims must be subject to debate and re-appraisal. It would also be wrong to forget, at any stage in the discussion, that recognising something as a right is only a first step towards ensuring the practical delivery of rights; no assumptions will be made at this stage about the link between the rhetoric of proclaiming rights and the realities of securing them in practice.

1. The right to be presumed innocent until convicted

This apparently simple right has a number of ramifications. Article 6.2 of the European Convention on Human Rights declares that "everyone charged with a criminal offence shall be presumed innocent until proved guilty according to law." The presumption of innocence, as it is usually termed, points in at least two different directions. It has reference to the treatment of suspects and defendants before and during the trial, insisting that such treatment must be consistent with respect for their innocence—one example of which is the presumption in favour of bail for persons charged with an offence, developed under Article 5.3 of the Convention.[26] It also has reference to the logistics of proof in criminal cases—which party must prove what—and this will be the focus of the discussion here.

The general principle, stated in English law and adopted in European human rights law, is that the prosecution should bear the burden of proving the accused's guilt, and that guilt should be proved to the standard "beyond reasonable doubt" rather than on a simple balance of probabilities.[27] One way of expressing this is that a defendant has the right to put the prosecution to proof, and should not be required to exculpate himself or otherwise disprove guilt just because he has been charged with an offence. Whether phrased as the presumption of innocence or as the principle of putting the prosecution to proof, the essence seems to reside in the relationship between the State and the citizen, and the idea of respect for the liberty of citizens. In the leading U.S. decision the Supreme Court asserted that it is:

> important in our free society that every individual going about his ordinary affairs have confidence that his government cannot adjudge him guilty of a criminal offense without convincing a proper fact-finder of his guilt with utmost certainty.[28]

This locates the justification for the presumption in the context of a citizen's legitimate expectations of how the State should behave towards him or her. If the citizen is to be respected as a rational and responsible individual, who may fairly expect to be able to plan ahead and to avoid the criminal justice system by behaving in conformity with the criminal law, it is wrong that the authorities of the State, with all their power, should be able not only to accuse people of crimes but then to require them to disprove their guilt. As the Supreme Court also said:

> the accused during a criminal prosecution has at stake interests of immense importance, both because of the possibility that he may lose his liberty upon conviction and because of the certainty that he would be stigmatized by the conviction.

This is moving towards the view that "the unintentional conviction of the innocent is a greater evil than the unintentional acquittal of the guilty,"[29] and that, although a system of criminal justice should strive to eliminate mistakes of both kinds, greater efforts should be made to avoid the particularly deep injustice done to an innocent citizen by a wrongful conviction. Thus, if one adds the great power of the State authorities to the considerable effects a conviction can have on a citizen, and places both in the context of the citizen as a responsible subject in a democratic system, it surely follows that the prosecution should bear the burden of proving guilt, and that it would be intolerable if courts were to operate with a presumption of guilt which the defendant had to strive to displace.[30] The presumption of innocence can therefore be justified on a combination of principled and instrumental rationales. The same can be said of requiring a high standard of proof in a criminal trial, such as "beyond reasonable doubt." To quote again from the U.S. Supreme Court in *Re Winship*, "a society that values the good name and freedom of every individual should not condemn a man for commission of a crime where there is reasonable doubt about his guilt."[31] This links to the proposition that to convict an innocent person is a fundamental moral harm which the State must strive to avoid if it is to show any respect for citizens as thinking members of society.[32] It is a fundamental moral harm because the misapplication of blame and public censure is a deep injustice, and also because the consequences of deprivation or restriction of liberty that may follow conviction would be unjustified.

However, there has to be a compromise, even in respect of so fundamental a right as the right of an innocent person not to be convicted, because a legal system that devoted maximum effort to eliminating all risk of wrongful conviction would exhaust massive resources which could and should be devoted to other socially important ends. In this way, one might find a justification for the "beyond reasonable doubt" standard: it takes seriously the right of the innocent not to be convicted, but does not demand the elimination of all doubts, a standard so high that it would also have the effect of reducing drastically the number of convictions of the guilty. This is not to say that all is well and that the present arrangements for proof are unassailable. There is much more that can and should be done to prevent the conviction of the innocent, separately from altering the standard of proof in criminal cases. The point is that we must strive for the best system that takes seriously the rights of the innocent, whilst also making some practical concessions to the social importance of convicting the guilty and of other goals such as health, education, housing and so forth.

What might the sceptic say about these principles? Few would argue in favour of a system which incorporates a presumption of guilt against anyone charged with an offence, requiring the accused to prove innocence. Some might wish to argue that prosecutors should only have to prove guilt on a balance of probabilities, on the basis that the "beyond reasonable doubt" standard imposes an unrealistically high threshold which leads to the acquittal of too many guilty people. The most likely response of the sceptic, however, would be one of "confession and avoidance", one that accepts the wisdom of placing a burden of proof beyond reasonable doubt on the prosecution but which argues that parts of the burden may properly be shifted to the defendant in certain types of case. This is a position evidently espoused by many parliamentarians and judges. For many years, criminal legislation has included "reverse onus" provisions, placing on the defendant the burden of proving certain matters. In some instances the defendant is assigned the burden of proving a defence, excuse or exemption, once the prosecution has proved that the elements of the offence itself are present. This may appear unobjectionable, until it is recalled that proving guilt means establishing the facts necessary to convict, that if the accused has a valid defence the prosecution will be unable to gain a conviction, and therefore that requiring a defendant to establish a defence is to lighten what should be the prosecutor's burden.

It is fair to expect the accused to adduce sufficient evidence to show that he may fall within a particular defence (known as the "evidential burden"), not least because it would be ridiculously disproportionate to expect the prosecution to negative every possible defence to the crime charged. But once a defence has been thus raised as a live issue it ought to fall to the prosecution to prove that it does not apply in this case, since that is an integral part of proving guilt (the overall "burden of persuasion").[33] Self-defence is a clear example of the proper approach: where a person is charged with a crime of violence, the prosecution does not have to negative self-defence unless the defendant adduces sufficient evidence to lay a foundation for it, in which case the prosecution bear the burden of disproving self-defence beyond a reasonable doubt. Thus the real concern is "not whether the accused must disprove an element to prove an excuse, but that an accused may be convicted while a reasonable doubt exists."[34]

Both Parliament and the judges, however, have frequently succumbed to the temptation to impose persuasive burdens on the defence. Summary offences almost invariably impose the burden on the accused of bringing himself within any defence, exemption or proviso to an offence;[35] and a combination of legislative provisions and judicial decisions has the effect of imposing burdens of the defence in many indictable offences too.[36] Parliament has fairly routinely imposed burdens of proof on the defendant, without seeking special justification, and in particular without addressing the argument that an evidential burden on the defence would be sufficient.[37] Recently, however, there is evidence of judicial and parliamentary willingness to scrutinise the justifications for taking the step of imposing a persuasive burden of proof on the defendant, a move prompted by Article 6.2 of the European Convention,[38] although not by the decisions of the Strasbourg Court.[39] The decision of the House of Lords in *Lambert*[40] is all the more powerful because the statutory provision was worded so as to impose the burden of proof on the defence and did so in the context of drugs legislation, but the House still held that it should be interpreted as imposing only an evidential burden on the defendant, so as not to violate the presumption of innocence. If this approach is followed, several other provisions will now have to be reinterpreted.[41]

2. The privilege against self-incrimination

We now turn to the privilege against self-incrimination, the essence of which is that citizens should not be coerced into producing evidence against themselves (the Latin maxim is *nemo debet prodere se ipsum*).[42] The privilege has theoretical connections with the presumption of innocence, insofar as that presumption embodies the principle of putting the prosecution to proof of guilt, for the reasons elaborated in the foregoing discussion.[43] The privilege against self-incrimination is declared in Article 14(3)(g) of the International Covenant on Civil and Political Rights, the right "not to be compelled to testify against himself or to confess guilt," and it is one of two closely linked rights—the other is the right of silence—which the Strasbourg Court has implied into Article 6, on the basis that the two rights are internationally recognised as lying at the heart of the notion of a fair trial.[44] The privilege against self-incrimination runs deeper than the right of silence: that right restricts the extent to which adverse inferences may be drawn from a failure to answer questions or to comment on statements, whereas the privilege restricts the extent to which a citizen can be placed under a duty to answer questions or to supply information. It runs deeper because the privilege concerns direct coercion applied to citizens to do certain things (*e.g.* a requirement to supply certain information, on pain of conviction and punishment for failure to do so), whereas the right of silence concerns only indirect coercion in the form of the possible drawing of adverse inferences from failure to speak. Yet the right and the privilege are closely connected, both in theory and in practice, and they are only separated here so as to enable a discussion of the range of forms of institutional pressure that may be placed on citizens by the criminal justice system.

The privilege against self-incrimination has been recognised by the Strasbourg Court as a way of ensuring that the prosecution "seek to prove their case against the accused without resort to evidence obtained through methods of coercion or oppression in defiance of the will of the accused."[45] This seems to mean that, although provisions requiring a person to answer questions in relation to a suspected crime do not necessarily violate the Convention, it would be a violation if the prosecution used the resulting evidence in a subsequent criminal trial.[46] However, the Court has now gone further than this, and has held that where a person refuses to answer questions and is convicted of an offence for that refusal, the existence of the offence itself amounts to a violation of the privilege against self-incrimination if the sentence for the offence is significant. Thus in *Heaney and McGuinness v. Ireland*[47] the Court unanimously held that the privilege had been breached by the conviction of the two applicants of an offence of refusing to give the police an account of their movements during a specified period, as required by an Irish statute on terrorism. They had both been sentenced to the maximum of six months' imprisonment, and this was held to have destroyed the very essence of the privilege. The degree of compulsion to speak was far too great. The Court went further: it reinforced an earlier decision[48] in which (a) the requirement was to produce documents, not to answer questions,[49] and (b) the penalty was financial (accumulating fines, which increased as time went by if the applicant refused to yield up the documents). This is not an isolated decision of the Court,[50] and it suggests that wherever there is a criminal offence of failure to answer questions or to supply information, the compatibility of that provision with the privilege against self-incrimination will be in doubt.

Why should the privilege against self-incrimination be honoured? It may be a "generally recognised international standard," but what are its moral and political credentials? One way of sharpening the search for its rationale is to consider what tends to be excluded from the ambit of the privilege. Thus in the leading case of *Saunders v. United Kingdom*,[51] the European Court of Human Rights stated that the privilege against self-incrimination is concerned primarily with "respecting the will of an accused person to remain silent," and that it:

> does not extend to the use in criminal proceedings of material which may be obtained from the accused through the use of compulsory powers but which has an existence independent of the will of the suspect such as, *inter alia*, documents acquired pursuant to a warrant, breath, blood and urine samples and bodily tissue for the purpose of DNA testing.[52]

What light does this distinction, which roughly corresponds with that drawn by the Supreme Court of the United States,[53] throw upon the justification for the privilege? Is there any reason why coerced speech should be protected, but not coerced submission to the taking of bodily samples? It could certainly be said that compulsory powers of the kind set out above would only be permitted where there were reasonable grounds to suspect the commission of an offence, but that might equally be required before a person were required to speak. Four possible reasons for treating the two situations differently might be given brief consideration here.

First, it is sometimes said that the privilege is necessary in order to protect each person's privacy, that is, their right to respect for their private life.[54] To force someone to speak is to require a person to articulate his or her own personal knowledge, impressions and secrets. This is inconsistent with proper respect for privacy, a right protected by Article 8 of the European Convention, but can it not equally be said that the right is violated by a coercive provision for the taking of a blood or urine sample? That amounts to an actual invasion of the person's body, which is surely within the private zone that any right to respect for private life should protect. It could be said that the privilege is concerned only with the protection of "mental privacy", but that begs the question "why?". There seems to be no convincing answer to this question at the level of principle: what emerges is the pragmatic consideration that almost all legal systems find it necessary to make provision for the compulsory taking of bodily samples in certain types of case.

A second rationale is that the privilege against self-incrimination is necessary to protect the autonomy of each individual. If the State wishes to prosecute a person for an offence, then it must prove its case. To place obligations on a citizen to assist the State in proving the case against him would not only be to fail to respect him as an autonomous subject,[55] but also be to undermine the presumption of innocence. Criminal conviction is a serious matter, and recognition of the values of liberty and autonomy of citizens requires proper respect for the presumption of innocence, which in turn tells against exerting pressure on citizens to incriminate themselves. This rationale has close affinities with the privacy argument; and, like that, it offers no means of regarding forced oral statements as unacceptable whilst compelled bodily samples are considered acceptable.

A third rationale, which draws strength from the first two but has a more instrumental bent, is that the privilege protects citizens from cruel choices which it is unfair to impose on them.[56] Without the privilege, a person would either succumb to the threat and answer the accusations or give the required information, or would decline to do so and then be liable to conviction, either for the offence of failing to answer or for the substantive offence by the drawing of adverse inferences. These choices are unfair, especially if the links with the presumption of innocence and the protection of privacy and autonomy are granted some force. Moreover, for the State to create these pressures to lie raises serious questions about the justifications for punishment in these cases[57]: it is not just that some will construct lies, but also that some will have difficulty admitting to themselves what they have done.

These three rationales, taken together, tend to support the privilege against self-incrimination by reference to a certain conception of the citizen's right to respect for his or her autonomy, and the concomitant belief that it would be an abuse of power for the State to have the power to question people under compulsory powers in order to obtain evidence with which to build cases against them. In that sense, the privilege draws strength from the presumption of innocence. However, it is not clear that these rationales can justify the distinction between allowing forced bodily samples whilst disallowing forced oral statements. The fourth possible rationale does claim to be able to do this. It is the so-called "anti-pooling rationale",[58] which uses the privilege as a way of trying to ensure that statements by guilty people are not confused with statements by innocent people. It thus applies the privilege wherever there is the possibility, and hence the temptation, of telling a lie. This does supply a justification for distinguishing between oral statements and bodily samples, inasmuch as the latter cannot be the subject of a lie. It also urges that the line be drawn between compelling a person to produce documents which have his or her signature on them (permissible, insofar as documents already exist) and compelling a person to give samples of hand-writing (not permissible, because of the opportunity for dissimulation).[59] The anti-pooling approach is claimed to "impose order on self-incrimination doctrine", by exempting from the doctrine "evidence known to exist at the time of its compelled production", such as bodily samples, but including within it all evidence and statements susceptible to manipulation by the maker.

> By making silence advantageous to guilty suspects, the right to silence helps the innocent as well as the guilty; without this right, the guilty would lack an incentive to separate themselves from the innocent; the unfortunate result would be a pooling of all suspects, which would decrease the credibility of the exonerating accounts of innocent suspects and defendants.[60]

The anti-pooling rationale differs from the others in that it is not grounded in deep principle but rather in empirically testable assumptions about behaviour, related to one of the primary purposes of the criminal justice system (to convict the guilty and acquit the innocent). It should therefore take its place alongside other instrumental rationales.

Ian Dennis argues that, since no legal system seems able to operate without making some inroads into the full privilege against self-incrimination, we should recognise that inroads or

21

exceptions will have to be made, and focus our attention on assessing the degree to which each of them is justified by reference to its capacity to produce reliable evidence and its preservation of as much of the principle as possible.[61] Certainly there should be no exceptions that infringe the substantive rights of suspects under the Convention, notably the absolute rights under Article 3 (no torture or inhuman or degrading conduct) and the qualified rights under Article 8 (respect for private life). Further than that, the questions about the scope and weight of the privilege itself remain.

The sceptic would emerge from the shadows at this stage. Having watched as all the deeper principles run into difficulties that make them less than wholly convincing, the sceptic might now take advantage of the shift to pragmatic arguments by contending that the operation of a safe society, which protects the interests of the law-abiding, makes it necessary to accept the creation of two levels of powers that run counter to the privilege against self-incrimination. At one level the case in favour of restricting the privilege in investigations of the most serious crime (including terrorism) would be pressed, on the basis that this is necessary if public safety is to be properly assured. This runs counter to the Court's decision in *Heaney and McGuinness v. Ireland*,[62] and of course it begs certain empirical questions about the gains reasonably to be expected from restricting the privilege, but sceptics would not be reluctant to press the argument. On a much lower level there are those, including some advocates of rights, who would argue that limited exceptions to the privilege should be allowed where the incursion is small and the social benefits large. A prime example to which this argument would be applied is the power to require samples of breath, blood or urine from suspects, or other samples for DNA purposes. Support for the notion that this is necessary for greater public protection might be derived from the prevalence of such powers among Western European nations. The same might be said of the power to require the owner of a motor vehicle to state who was driving it at a given time, and the power to require a citizen to divulge the amount and provenance of her or his earnings. Without insisting on some such duties as these, law enforcement and therefore public protection would be hampered unduly. Some would take the same view of compulsion to make returns of income and assets to tax authorities. There are those who argue that, if rights are not to be given a bad name, concessions should be made on pragmatic grounds in these fairly obvious types of case. This would leave those supporters of the privilege with the problem of how to ensure that the privilege is not overwhelmed by exceptions of this kind; others would rather not accept the exceptions in the first place. This is a debate that has never received much attention in British public policy.

3. The right of silence

The privilege against self-incrimination is supposed to safeguard citizens against laws that force them to give information or answer questions, on pain of criminal conviction. We now move to the right of silence, and to laws that permit adverse inferences to be drawn from a person's failure to answer questions or to offer an explanation for certain facts. The basic issues are the same as for the privilege against self-incrimination: should a suspect be able to sit back and leave the prosecution to prove guilt, without any help from him? Or is it fair to allow the court to draw adverse inferences from a suspect's failure to tell the police about facts on which reliance is later placed in his defence?

Before going further into this controversial issue, it is necessary to point out the difference between answering police questions and responding to the prosecution's case in court. When the case comes to court, the evidence for the prosecution is set out openly, and any pressure on the accused to respond should derive chiefly from the evidence presented in the reasonably controlled setting of the courtroom. English law permits adverse inferences from an accused's failure to give evidence when the prosecution has made out a case to answer, having attained the required degree of proof of all the key elements of the crime charged[63]; but even in that situation the defendant is still free to remain silent, to call other witnesses on his behalf and then to put the prosecution to proof. In contrast, when a person is being questioned by the police, it may not be clear exactly what is being alleged, and on what evidence it is based, and there is the possibility that the whole purpose of questioning the suspect is to generate the evidence with which to bring a prosecution.[64] Thus, if we focus on the pre-trial investigation, the right of silence can be supported on both principled and instrumental grounds. The reasons of principle in favour of the right of silence are the same as those supporting the privilege against self-incrimination and discussed in section 2 above— protecting privacy, respecting autonomy, shielding defendants from cruel choices, and providing incentives which better enable a court to distinguish between the innocent and the guilty. These reasons are particularly powerful when applied to vulnerable and confused defendants: those who are innocent may well be at a disadvantage if adverse inferences from silence are possible, because they may have the choice between giving explanations or testimony that might not do them justice,[65] or suffering adverse inferences unless the defence lawyer is successful in persuading the court that their condition constituted a reasonable excuse for failure to answer questions. Since we are discussing the right to silence when questioned by the police, and questioning in a police station imposes well-documented psychological pressures, these dangers are not confined to a small group of suspects.

Once again, there is a strong link to the presumption of innocence: the right of silence draws not only upon the fundamental value of not convicting innocent people but also on the value of accuracy. Any incentive to answer police questions increases the likelihood of confessions, both true and false ones. Many people find it hard to believe that someone would confess to a crime he or she had not committed, but the Royal Commission on Criminal Justice pointed out in 1993 that "there is now a substantial body of research which shows that there are at least four distinct categories of false confession"[66]; and a majority of the Royal Commission opposed adverse inferences from silence because of the risk of more false statements:

> The majority of us believe that the possibility of an increase in the convictions of the guilty is outweighed by the risk that the extra pressure on suspects to talk in the police station and the adverse inferences invited if they do not may result in more convictions of the innocent ... It is the less experienced and more vulnerable suspects against whom the threat of adverse comments would be likely to be more damaging. There are too many cases of improper pressures being brought to bear on suspects in police custody, even where the safeguards of PACE and the codes of practice have supposedly been in force, for the majority to regard this with equanimity.[67]

As is well known, the Royal Commission's arguments did not persuade the then Government, which took the sceptic's view that the right of silence placed too great a burden on the prosecution, and that those who took advantage of it were predominantly guilty people, especially "professional criminals" who could cover their tracks and could "silence" others with their threats. These were the reasons given for Parliament's enactment of the Criminal Justice and Public Order Act 1994, sections 34–38, permitting adverse inferences from silence in certain situations.

Since then, however, the United Kingdom has lost a number of cases in Strasbourg on this issue. The European Court of Human Rights has held that the right of silence forms part of the fundamental right to a fair trial enshrined in Article 6, and its judgments on the relevant rules in Northern Ireland and in England and Wales have been largely negative. Thus:

> the Court considers that the extent to which adverse inferences can be drawn from an accused's failure to respond to police questioning must necessarily be limited. While it may no doubt be expected in most cases that innocent persons would be willing to co-operate with the police in explaining that they were not involved in any suspected crime, there may be reasons why in a specific case an innocent person would not be prepared to do so.[68]

Obvious examples of those reasons would be a desire to shield a friend or family member, or a desire to conceal some discreditable (but not necessarily criminal) fact. It is therefore not always an accurate inference from silence that the suspect is guilty. But the stronger point to be made is that it is not fair to suspects to allow those inferences to be drawn: it is a form of indirect compulsion. One of the implications of the right to legal advice is that a suspect might in those circumstances be advised not to answer (certain) questions from the police. The right to legal advice would be significantly impaired if a suspect were not free to act on proper advice, without suffering a detriment (such as adverse inferences). So it was that the European Court of Human Rights held that:

> The very fact that an accused is advised by his lawyer to maintain his silence must also be given appropriate weight by the domestic court. There may be good reason why such advice may be given. The applicants in the instant case state that they held their silence on the strength of their solicitor's advice that they were unfit to answer questions.[69]

This last point illustrates the need to pay attention to the range of situations in which police questioning may take place. Thus the Strasbourg Court has held that there may be circumstances in which it will be fair to draw adverse inferences from a failure to offer an explanation. While the Court has clearly stated that the reason for upholding the two rights is "the protection of the accused against improper compulsion by the authorities, thereby contributing to the avoidance of miscarriages of justice and to the fulfilment of the aims of Article 6," the rights have not been regarded as absolute—rather as capable of yielding to circumstances that are particularly compelling. Thus, acceptance that the right of silence is a generally recognised international standard "cannot and should not prevent that the accused's silence, in circumstances which clearly call for an explanation from him, be taken into account in assessing the persuasiveness of the evidence adduced by the prosecution."[70] Such factors as the presence of incriminating fibres on clothing, or the suspect's presence at the scene of the crime, may properly lead to adverse inferences if no explanation is advanced by the defence.[71] In these instances, it appears, the drawing of an inference may be necessary to forge the link between weighty circumstantial evidence and the accused's guilt; and, on "common sense" grounds, the Court regards the inference as permissible if no plausible explanation for the strongly incriminating evidence is forthcoming. It does, however, represent a clear limitation on the right of silence, which some would oppose on principle.[72]

This restriction on the right which the Strasbourg Court recognised from the outset may be thought to give some support to the sceptic's view. It is noticeable, however, that in recognising these exceptional cases the Court based its reasoning on the nature of the evidential situation: it is the perceived strength of the apparently incriminating evidence that is taken as a justification for overriding the general right not to have adverse inferences drawn from failure to offer a plausible explanation. This should be distinguished sharply from the argument that it is the seriousness of the crime with which the accused is charged, or the complexity of investigating it, which justifies restrictions on the right. It is only in the former types of case where the Strasbourg approach gives greater weight to what it regards as the promotion of accuracy, as a justification for this limited overriding of the considerations of autonomy and privacy and the potential for abuse of power that generally support the right of silence.

4. *The right to legal aid and assistance*

Would it be right for a person who has been arrested and taken to a police station for questioning to be refused access to a legal adviser? Of course, many people detained for questioning will not want a lawyer. They will simply want to clear the matter up as quickly as possible, but the question is whether they should have a right to a lawyer if they want one; or, put differently, whether the police should be able to deny them the opportunity to take legal advice. Various points can be made here: that one suspect faced with two or more police officers is relatively powerless; that suspects in police custody are at a significant psychological disadvantage, and have been known to say things that are untrue, simply in order to secure early release or for other reasons; and that some suspects are gullible or vulnerable, and need protection against the wiles of professional investigators.[73] Probably the most powerful argument is that, since the questioning relates to a possible criminal offence, there is a great deal at stake for the individual citizen and it is therefore appropriate that he or she should have the right to take legal advice. That argument becomes overwhelming when the law permits adverse inferences from the suspect's failure to answer questions or to explain apparently incriminating facts. Although English law on inferences from silence has been modified as a result of Strasbourg decisions,[74] there are still various situations in which inferences may properly be drawn, and that makes it particularly important that a suspect should have access to a lawyer at the outset of police questioning.[75] In many European jurisdictions a suspect is not entitled to have a lawyer present during police questioning, even though there may be provision for access to a lawyer outside the interrogation,[76] but this is usually counterbalanced by a right of silence which does not allow for the drawing of adverse inferences.

The sceptic might challenge this right by arguing that legal advisers might obstruct the investigation, and might even present a security risk. The latter point requires a procedure for checking that the fear of a security risk has substance in relation to the particular legal adviser, but it still may not be a good reason for denying access to any lawyer at a time when a person is being questioned on matters that might affect the case against him.[77] As for the potential of legal advisers to "obstruct" an investigation, this may be their proper role, insofar as they may decide to advise a suspect not to answer questions if the police do not have, or have not declared to the lawyer, a sufficient basis for asking them. For this, the lawyers need to be properly trained and to obey ethical codes; if they do this conscientiously, that may indeed place obstacles in the path of the police, but those obstacles are supported by other rights discussed below.

The argument for legal assistance is no less strong when a case comes to court. Courts and lawyers operate with a degree of technical complexity and jargon. Moreover, the police and prosecution have considerable public resources at their command, compared with those of most individual defendants, and this supplies an extra reason for legal representation. Then the principle of equality before the law points to the inequity of allowing an individual's financial resources to determine

27

whether or not legal assistance is available. Thus there are two mutually supporting justifications for legal aid for defendants in non-minor criminal cases—that it would be unjust if the prosecution were represented by a lawyer and the defence were not, because of the defendant's inability to afford legal representation; and that it would be unjust if a distinction were drawn between rich and poor defendants, such that the former could pay for legal assistance whereas the latter were left unable to afford legal aid. These consequences would be unjust because they might impair a defendant's ability to mount a proper defence, and might therefore risk convictions of the innocent. The argument is not for precise "equality of arms" between prosecution and defence, but for recognition that defendants are entitled to such legal assistance as enables them to make a proper defence.

The sceptic may suggest that this argument, though fine in principle, may well lead to undesired consequences of different kinds—the self-interest of lawyers may lead some to prolong trials, and others to influence defendants in the direction of plea bargains which are not in the defendant's best interests. This is a realm of lawyers' activity which is still not adequately regulated[78]—a separate issue from the one under consideration here, but no less important. Moreover, the self-interest of some lawyers is a point which may tell in either direction, in that certain defence lawyers may adopt strategies of co-operation with the police which might place the client at some disadvantage in order to maintain the lawyer's standing with the police.[79]

5. The right to be brought promptly before a court

If a suspect is being investigated by the police, should they be allowed to hold him until their investigations have finished? There are two reasons why not. First, assuming that the suspect is under arrest or otherwise in detention, he is being deprived of his liberty. Whilst it may be right for a person to suffer some loss of liberty if there are reasonably founded suspicions against him, since otherwise it would be too difficult for the investigation of crime to take place, this should be for as short a period as possible. In other words, a right to liberty (freedom of movement) should be recognised; that right should be subordinated to the exigencies of investigation where there are reasonable (objective) grounds for suspicion; but the period of subordination should be as short as possible, out of respect for the fundamental right which is being curtailed. Secondly, and relatedly, it should not be for the police alone to determine the length of detention (deprivation of liberty) without charge. As the Strasbourg Court has put it, there must be "judicial control of interferences by the executive with the individual's right to liberty."[80] Thus the suspect must either be released, or be charged and brought before a court "promptly". What, for these purposes, is promptly? English law allows up to 24 hours, with provision for extensions up to a maximum of 96 hours where the arrest is for a "serious arrestable offence" (the extensions beyond 36 hours requiring the approval of a court). The European Court of Human Rights also seems to regard four days as the maximum period of detention before a person is brought to court.[81]

It might be said that a court hearing in these circumstances is unlikely to be a potent safeguard for the suspect, against being detained without sufficient cause, since the court is unlikely to be in a good position to test the prosecution's submission. Where a suspect has had access to legal advice, it may be possible for the defence lawyer to force some assessment of the strength of the arguments. However, in practice the English system is loaded against the suspect. The police tend to make considerable use of their informal power to bring someone to a police station to "help with their inquiries," and to rely on the suspect's ignorance of his or her freedom to leave: arrest is often reserved for serious cases, for suspects who know their rights, or for suspects who no longer wish to "help the police with their inquiries." Research also shows that the criteria for detention are not applied strictly, and that the custody sergeant invariably accepts the arresting officer's word on this and other issues.[82] Moreover, detention in a police station is rarely a pleasant experience, since the facilities are often poor and the detainee is relatively powerless.[83] These and other practical problems show that even the minimum rights declared by the European Convention may not guarantee much protection for the citizen in the hands of the police.

Despite this, a sceptic might argue that the maximum period of 96 hours is too short for really major incidents, especially in alleged terrorist cases. If the public is to receive adequate protection, the police must be allowed a much freer hand. This was the essence of the British Government's response to the European Court of Human Rights decision in *Brogan v. United Kingdom*,[84] which held that the detention of suspected terrorists for period of over four, and up to seven, days without access to a court, as permitted by the then anti-terrorism legislation, violated their Article 5 rights. The Government responded by taking the significant step of entering a derogation from Article

5 in respect of the anti-terrorism legislation, citing the Northern Ireland conflict as a "public emergency threatening the life of the nation" under Article 15.[85] The position has been changed by the Terrorism Act 2000 in two major ways: first, although detention of suspects for seven days without charge remains possible, there are provisions requiring the detainee to be brought before a judge and allowing representations from the defence—provisions which may or may not satisfy Article 5 of the Convention; and secondly, the definition of terrorism is broadened considerably by section 1 of the 2000 Act so as to cover a wide range of acts of violence or property damage motivated by ideological causes.[86] In the wake of the events of September 11, 2001, the Government has again entered a derogation from Article 5 in respect of the extreme measure of detention without trial, introduced as part of the package of measures in the Anti-Terrorism, Crime and Security Act 2001. The need for this, and its lawfulness, are both contestable.[87] The possible problems do not end there. There is the further danger that exceptional powers of this kind will be extended to other forms of serious crime, a possibility rendered all the more real by the elastic definition of terrorism in the 2000 Act.

6. *The right to release pending trial*

Once a person has been charged and brought before a court, there should be a right to release before trial. It would fail to respect the presumption of innocence if people could lose their liberty merely on the basis that they have been charged by police and prosecutors with an offence. Deprivation of liberty is fundamentally problematic, as Article 5 of the European Convention establishes. There are exceptions to the prohibition on deprivation of liberty, one of which arises after conviction and sentence by a competent court, but the right to bail, *i.e.* to release pending trial, is less strong than most of the other rights considered here, since it is widely recognised that it should give way to particular "public interest" considerations. Although these considerations vary somewhat from country to country, four of them have been recognised by the European Court of Human Rights—the risk that the accused will fail to appear for trial, a reason connected with the proper functioning of the criminal justice system; the risk that the accused will interfere with witnesses if released, a reason which calls for the protection of victims and other witnesses,[88] as well as supporting the integrity of the system; the risk that the accused will commit serious offences if released, a reason which seems to derive from the State's overall duty to prevent crime; and the risk that releasing the accused would lead to public disorder, a risk heightened where there has been a notorious crime attracting much publicity, and a reason also related to the State's overall duty to prevent crime.

Why should a person's right to liberty give way so easily to "public interest" considerations, when we do not dispense easily (if at all) with other rights such as the right to legal advice? There seems to be an assumption that the State's duty to prevent crime justifies this: but the courts would not imprison a person who has not committed an offence if the police simply came and requested it, so in what way are these cases different? The answer seems to be that the application of the presumption of innocence is diminished by the decision to prosecute. This in turn assumes that the basis for arrest, charge and prosecution can reliably be thought to indicate a prima facie case against the accused. However, this seems doubtful both in law and in practice. In law the requirements of "reasonable grounds" for suspicion have become very thin in both domestic and European law.[89] In practice the evidence shows that decisions to arrest and charge may not always be based on the objective criteria suggested by the requirement of "reasonable grounds"[90]; and at the first remand hearing the police file will be incomplete, which means that the prosecution will not have been able to scrutinise the evidence. Thus the court will not be in a good position to assess the strength of the case; indeed, it may be some weeks before a reasonably full police file becomes available. If there is substance in these reflections, it suggests the need for a more critical look at the first three approved reasons for depriving charged but untried people of their liberty. The fourth reason may be regarded as even more doubtful, insofar as it purports to justify the detention of one person by reference to the probable criminal behaviour of others, rather than warning those others of the consequences of breaking the law.

The sceptic would press the "public interest" considerations strongly, arguing that the general presumption of innocence must be displaced where officials have conscientiously concluded that the evidence is such that a charge is warranted. Naturally it will take time for a case file to be completed, especially if forensic science tests need to be carried out, but it is too great a risk to release all defendants while these investigations continue. This is one sphere in which, it is urged, practical dangers dictate the need for preventive custody. The response to that may concede the argument for some uses of preventive custody, but insist on more rigorous examination of the justifications in each case, particularly where there is reliance on

generalised and stereotypical reasoning rather than par-
ticularised evidence.

7. The right to disclosure of documents

Should a defendant be able to find out what evidence and what
statements the prosecution are relying on? In some legal systems this is a question that makes little sense, because there is a
figure such as an examining judge who builds up a dossier on
the defendant which is open to inspection by defence lawyers as
well as prosecutors. In the English system it is a question with
several ramifications. The basic principle of prosecution disclosure has now been accepted in the Criminal Procedure and
Investigations Act 1996, but the reasoning behind this has never
been entirely clear. It seems that the European principle of
"equality of arms" is broadly accepted—the notion that it is fair
if the defence are able to have access to prosecution evidence, so
as to compensate for the disparity in resources and to raise them
to a roughly equal position. This stops short of accepting the
argument that the police gather evidence as trustees, rather than
"for the prosecution", so that it does not belong to the prosecution in any way, but is rather a form of public property that
should be open to the defence as well. So long as the "trustee-
ship" doctrine is not accepted, there remains the risk of repeat-
ing the notorious "miscarriage of justice" cases uncovered
around 1990, many of which stemmed from the failure of the
police or prosecution to disclose to the defence material that
would assist them.[91] Thus the defendant's right to disclosure has
strong links with the presumption of innocence, as well as with
the right of a person charged with a criminal offence to have
proper "facilities for the preparation of his defence."[92]

Whatever the basis for prosecution disclosure, claims are
often made that it should be subject to various limitations. The
European Court of Human Rights regards it as essential to the
right to a fair trial that "the prosecution authorities should
disclose to the defence all material evidence in their possession
for or against the accused"[93], but has recognised that:

> the entitlement to disclosure of all relevant evidence is not an
> absolute right. In any criminal proceedings there may be competing
> interests, such as national security or the need to protect witnesses at
> risk of reprisals or keep secret police methods of investigating crime,
> which must be weighed against the rights of an accused. In some
> cases it may be necessary to withhold certain evidence from the
> defence so as to preserve the fundamental rights of another individ-
> ual or to safeguard an important public interest. However, only such

measures restricting the rights of the defence which are strictly necessary are permissible under Article 6(1). Moreover, in order to ensure that the accused receives a fair trial, any difficulties caused to the defence by a limitation on its rights must be sufficiently counter-balanced by the procedures followed by the judicial authorities.[94]

The final words of this quotation are significant: it is not simply that the right to disclosure can be "balanced away" whenever there is a countervailing public interest. The right must be maintained so far as possible; exceptions can only be permitted in limited circumstances; and when an exception is recognised, its scope must be kept to the minimum and the defence must be compensated for it in some way. Requirements of this kind indicate a possible way of both recognising public interest arguments and continuing to show respect for rights.

The sceptic would emphasise the pragmatic reasons for restricting the obligations of disclosure. These concern the large amount of documentation gathered in some cases: as the Attorney General's Guidelines of 2000 assert, one purpose of the 1996 Act is to "ensure that material is not disclosed which overburdens the participants in the trial process, diverts attention from the relevant issues, leads to unjustifiable delay, and is wasteful of resources."[95] Another pragmatic reason is the importance of preserving the anonymity of police informants and undercover officers, a matter that can be ventilated in the context of an application for public interest immunity but which may be of more general concern to the prosecution. The Strasbourg Court has recognised this second line of justification, as noted earlier, but the first set of pragmatic reasons remains a matter of controversy. In this country it is police officers who have the primary task of taking decisions in relation to primary disclosure, and prosecutors who have the task of checking their decisions and authorising disclosure. Even if this is an appropriate arrangement—and there are strong reasons of principle for saying that the police are too partisan to be granted this task— the two sets of participants have not always performed well in this respect,[96] and the response to the sceptic would be that the whole structure of the 1996 Act calls for principled reassessment.

8. *The right to confront witnesses*

This is a reconstruction of a right contained in Article 6(3)(d) of the Convention: the right "to examine or have examined witnesses against him." What it has been taken to mean is that it is a defendant's right to have the prosecution witnesses examined before a judicial officer with the defendant and a defence lawyer present. The rationale seems to be that it is essential for the defence to be able to put questions to those witnesses by way of cross-examination, on the assumption that cross-examination is an important tool for testing reliability and truthfulness, and also to be able to observe the witnesses' demeanour during questioning, on the assumption that these physical signs can be interpreted as providing evidence of the truth or falsehood of what they say. These assumptions are open to considerable debate,[97] but they lie at the root of adversarial criminal procedure. Taken together, the right to an adversarial hearing and the principle of equality of arms are central to the notion of a fair trial under the Convention,[98] and they underpin the right to confrontation. In the Convention the right is not expressed as having any exceptions, unlike (for example) the right to trial in public. However, the Strasbourg Court has upheld the screening or the anonymity of witnesses in exceptional circumstances such as well-founded fears of intimidation and the special vulnerability of certain witnesses. Such cases may be analysed as presenting the courts with a conflict between the rights of the defendant and the rights of witnesses, the latter rights being derived from the right of every individual to respect for private life protected by Article 8 (since the Convention contains no direct reference to the rights of victims and other witnesses). The Court has held that the conflict should be resolved in a way that recognises and values both sets of rights:

> If the anonymity of witnesses is maintained, the defence will be faced with difficulties which criminal proceedings should not normally involve. Accordingly, the Court has recognised that in such cases Article 6(1) taken together with Article 6(3)(d) of the Convention requires that the handicaps under which the defence labours be sufficiently counterbalanced by the procedures followed by the judicial authorities.[99]

The same accommodation has been made in cases where the prosecution has relied on the written statement of a witness too ill to attend court or to make a further oral statement.[100] However, in all cases in which Article 6(3)(d) has been thus qualified, the Court has insisted that a conviction cannot be upheld if it is based "wholly or mainly" on the non-compliant evidence.[101]

The sceptic would wish to go further in accommodating the needs of the prosecution and assuring the protection of witnesses, by making extensive provision for the use of video-link evidence, screening and anonymity in appropriate trials. Pointing also to the rather excessive claims made for the effectiveness of cross-examination and of observing the demeanour of the witness, the sceptic would suggest that greater use should be made of written statements and of the taking of evidence on commission. All these measures would advance law enforcement and the protection of witnesses,[102] it might be claimed, whilst depriving the defendant of very little real protection. The response would involve a re-assertion of the merits of an adversarial hearing with oral evidence, as the paradigm of a fair trial.

9. The right to be tried on evidence not obtained by violation of fundamental rights

This is a controversial right. It is not contained in the Convention as such; there are signs of its recognition in some decisions and not in others. It is accepted in English law to some degree, but not as a general proposition. The central case, on which there seems to be agreement, is that where evidence is obtained by torture or inhuman or degrading conduct, contrary to Article 3 of the Convention, a trial would be rendered unfair within the meaning of Article 6 if that evidence were relied upon by the prosecution.[103] This is hardly surprising, since Article 3 has been treated as a genuinely absolute right, with no exceptions based on any manner of public policy considerations or allegedly conflicting rights of other individuals. Yet it does raise a question: since the evidence now exists, why not admit it at the trial, and deal separately with the official who broke the law in obtaining it, for example by prosecuting him and also allowing the suspect to sue for damages for breach of the Convention right? Two points may be made in answer to this. First, it seems contradictory for one organ of the State, the courts, to take advantage of a breach of the law by another organ of the State, a law enforcement officer. So far as police conduct is concerned, those who enforce the law should also obey the law. In respect of the courts, it would be an added affront to basic rule-of-law values if they were to act on evidence obtained, not just by a breach of domestic law, but through a breach of a right fundamental enough to be declared in the European Convention. Secondly, it is now well established that the right to a fair trial extends to the fairness of pre-trial procedures, notably the obtaining of evidence by means of entrapment,[104] and is not restricted by the boundaries of the actual court proceedings.

Strong as these arguments may appear, they are not widely accepted. The idea of a fair trial under the Convention seems not to be firmly connected to violations of other rights. Whereas a breach of Article 3 will make it unfair to rely on a resulting confession, it seems that a breach of a defendant's Article 8 rights (for example, by listening in to his conversations without authorisation to do so) will not necessarily render it unfair to rely on the resulting evidence.[105] The only ways of reconciling the two rulings are to argue that the Article 3 right is stronger and more fundamental (in Convention terms) than the Article 8 right, or that Article 3 is more centrally concerned with criminal procedure than Article 8, and that the line is rightly drawn between the two. If one protests that a line should not be drawn at all, arguing that the violation of a Convention right ought to be sufficient to rule the evidence out, various consequentialist reasons are pressed forward. If reliable evidence exists, it would be a pity not to use it, and to risk the acquittal of a guilty person. For an acquittal in those circumstances is no better, and possibly worse for public confidence in the courts than acting on evidence which has been obtained by violation of a fundamental human right. However, these arguments are not necessarily persuasive. If the purpose of the Convention is to guarantee individuals protection from having their rights breached, it is surely appropriate that they should not be placed at a disadvantage in consequence of that breach.

The sceptic might argue that the public confidence argument is overdone, since confidence is probably less likely to be undermined by a court acting on unlawfully obtained evidence than by the acquittal of a defendant solely on the ground that the evidence was obtained by breach of a Convention right. The proper way to deal with such breaches is to allow the defendant a remedy in damages against the errant official, and to prosecute that official if an offence was committed, rather than to upset a trial where the reliability of the evidence is not in question.[106] The response would be to put the point again about adherence to rule-of-law values. What moral standing would a court have if it proceeded to a conviction on the basis of evidence obtained by a violation of a right that it purported to recognise as fundamental?

10. The right not to be placed in double jeopardy

The reasons for recognising this right are not difficult to find. If the State with all its resources and power were allowed to bring repeated prosecutions against a person for the same offence, this would be objectionable as "subjecting him to embarrassment, expense and ordeal and compelling him to live in a continuing state of anxiety and insecurity, as well as enhancing the possibility that even though innocent he may be found guilty."[107] Other subsidiary justifications for the right are the importance of finality and the promotion of efficient prosecution practice.[108] However, there are obvious problems about adherence to a principle of "no re-trials for the same offence": one is how to determine whether the offence is (essentially) the same, and another is whether it must be held that every reason for halting a criminal trial, or reversing a conviction on appeal, ought to result in the termination of proceedings for ever. Setting aside the former "technical" objection for the moment, how should the latter questions be answered? There could be a variety of reasons (*e.g.* inappropriate remarks by a juror, misdirection by the judge) for wishing to order a re-trial. Should all such re-trials be held incompatible with the right not to be placed in double jeopardy? The rationale offered for the double jeopardy rule is partly the adverse psychological effect on individuals subjected to repeated prosecutions, and partly the control of abuse of power. It seems that, if the decision to hold a re-trial is a fairly immediate result of either a halted trial or an overturned conviction, most countries recognise that this should not be a bar to a second trial—the argument presumably being that this is not an abuse of State power, and that the psychological pressures arising from what is effectively the prolongation of the trial process are not so great as to outweigh the public interest in having the defendant made subject to a properly-conducted trial. Where the decision to order a re-trial is based on some fault or alleged fault of the defendant, notably through intimidation of witnesses, a re-trial is surely right in principle. Where the fault in the original trial was that of the judge or other official, one might argue that a citizen should have to accept the burden of being subjected to one re-trial (but probably not more).

The European Convention recognises a further exception to what it terms "the right not to be tried or punished twice", stating that the right:

> shall not prevent the re-opening of the case in accordance with the law and penal procedure of the State concerned, if there is new evidence or newly discovered facts . . . which could affect the outcome of the case.[109]

This provision includes new means of proof relating to previous findings, and it covers re-opening of the case on the application of either the prosecution or the defence. Many European systems already have such a provision in their domestic law,[110] and the Law Commission has recently proposed the introduction of a similar exception into English law in cases of murder.[111] There has been provision since 1996 for the referral of convictions by the Criminal Cases Review Commission to the Court of Appeal for re-assessment, but no procedure for dealing with allegedly mistaken acquittals. The Law Commission's proposal would mean that a murder acquittal several years earlier could be revisited if the prosecution obtained significant new evidence, such as a DNA match from an article found at the scene. The result would be that an acquitted defendant would remain in jeopardy of a further trial: presumably the argument is that this should only prey on the minds of those who are in fact guilty, who are not entitled to be left psychologically at peace on this matter, although others might perhaps fear an unwarranted re-opening of their case.

The sceptic is likely to rejoice in the exceptions recognised by the Convention, and probably to urge English law to take full advantage of the exception in the Convention (rather than restricting it to murder). It is unlikely that prosecutors would wish to launch a second prosecution in many cases, but much depends on the drafting of the "new evidence" provision which would allow a further prosecution. Insofar as that is restrictively drafted, the sceptic would wish to see greater leeway for prosecutors and a reduced emphasis on the right. However, the basic justifications for the right remain persuasive, and there are strong arguments in favour of the restrictive English approach.

E.   CONFLICTING GOALS, CONFLICTING PRESSURES

The discussion in this lecture has shown how these fairly basic issues about criminal procedure and evidence can be approached from at least two very different standpoints: that of human rights, under the European Convention; and that of the sceptic, whose overriding concern is for what is termed "public safety." Different aspects of these conflicting perspectives will be examined further in the two coming lectures; for the present, we may conclude the present discussion with a few remarks about public safety, and a summary of the conflicting goals of criminal justice policy.

(i) *Public safety*

The assurance of public safety is prominent in all statements of official criminal justice policy: the Home Office's key statement of aims is to work towards "a safe, just and tolerant society," with safety placed first. Safety ought to be interpreted as a broad concept: in human rights discussions, it is important to recognise that it is not just safety from the deeds of other citizens but also safety from the unlawful use of power by officials that should be the focus of attention. In either context, safety is probably taken to relate to the risk of being subjected to criminal harm. It is natural for all citizens to be concerned about the risk of violence, but is this an increasing risk?

The overall figures for recorded crime in the ten years from 1989 to 1998–9 show a rise from 3.9 million to 4.5 million, but that does not tell the whole story, even allowing for the fact that those statistics only include crimes that are reported by the public and recorded by the police.[112] Those ten years saw the recorded crime rate rise sharply from 1989 to peak at 5.6 million in 1992, and since then there has been a significant decline of some 7–8 per cent per year. The 1998–9 figure of 4.5 million therefore shows a great fall in recorded crimes since 1992. However, this fall is attributable largely to significant reductions in reported thefts and burglaries. It masks an increase throughout the 1990s (though dipping in the last two years[113]) of the figures for four types of crime which have a bearing on public safety:

	1989	1992	1998–9
Violence	177,000	201,800	230,800
[*serious violence*	*13,900*	*17,800*	*26,900]*
Sexual offences	29,700	29,500	34,900
Robbery	33,200	52,900	66,200
Drug offences	7,800	13,800	21,300
Offences with firearms[114]	5,289	9,023	7,408

Unfortunately, these figures[115] are not particularly helpful for our purposes. They do indicate that all four classes of offence have shown overall increases, despite the general downward trend of recorded crime. But none of the categories is adequate to meet the criterion of "serious crime", save that of "serious violence". Sexual offences include not only the serious offence of rape, which has shown a sharp increase, but also offences of indecent assault which may be more or less serious. Many robberies are serious, but some of the offences recorded in this category involve little in the way of violence or threats, and the category of drug offences includes possession, which accounts for some nine-tenths of the total. As a result, the figure cannot be used as an indicator of the growth in drug trafficking on a large scale. Moreover, there are no separate figures for organised crime, which is often identified as a major threat to law and order and to public safety.

Although the figures are unable to offer a sharply focused picture of the risk to public safety, it would be fair to infer from them that the risk of serious violence is not decreasing and is probably increasing. There are, however, two further questions one might ask about public safety. One is whether the image of increased vulnerability to attack by strangers is itself an accurate one. The activities of organised crime are depicted as violent, and robberies usually involve attacks by strangers. But many offences of violence and sexual offences are committed by family members, "friends" and acquaintances rather than by strangers. For example, in 62 per cent of homicide offences in the last ten years the victim was acquainted with the suspect[116]; a recent study of reported rapes showed that 43 per cent of offenders were intimates of the victim, a further 45 per cent were acquaintances, and only 12 per cent were strangers.[117] This is not to suggest that any of these offences were less serious because of the existence of a prior relationship, but simply to make the point that the objective risk to "public safety" might not be found where many people think it is to be found. A second question concerns people's fears of serious crime: there is much debate about the extent to which fear and risk are out of step, and some groups of people have fears of crime that run well ahead of the objective risks. This is not the place to enter into the details of that debate.[118] However, it is possible that some of the public statements about threats to public safety refer to, or even generate, fears that do not correspond to the objective risks. The conclusion of this paragraph, then, is that there may be gaps between beliefs and realities about risks to public safety. This is not to deny that there are real risks to public safety, or that it is worth taking measures to try to reduce those risks.

Whether those preventive measures should rely significantly on court sentences is difficult to say. Because so few offences are reported, of those not all are recorded, and then only around a quarter are "cleared up", the proportion of offences that result in the conviction of the offender is estimated to be around 3 per cent.[119] The proportion is likely to be higher, perhaps around 15–16 per cent, for the more serious sexual and violent offences,[120] but even if one in six offenders are convicted and sentenced it would seem that the potential of the court system for preventing crime is somewhat blunted. It is true that reports of the sentences imposed on that small percentage of offenders may generate a greater general deterrent effect, but that would depend on a whole chain of causes and effects—including newspaper and television reporting, internalisation by potential offenders, and then the potency of that deterrent effect over a relatively low detection rate and other social pressures—which need to be carefully investigated rather than taken for granted.[121] In view of the known figures, it would be easy to over-estimate the preventive effect of those few sentences.

The 1990s, however, have seen two major changes which some might interpret as supporting the thesis that changes in sentencing levels have some general preventive effect, despite the relatively small proportion of offenders sentenced, and the even smaller proportion of offenders sentenced to custody (some 0.3 per cent of all known indictable offences result in a custodial sentence).[122] Thus between 1993 and 1999 the prison population rose by over 50 per cent, and the proportionate use of custody by the courts also rose by about a half, from 14.9 to 23.4 per cent. On the other hand, this repressive mood in Parliament and in the courts was accompanied by a decline in the rate of recorded crime after 1992, a decline which at first was confined to property offences but which by the end of the decade was beginning to appear in the less numerous categories of violent and sexual crimes. Some have argued that this establishes a relationship of cause and effect: the imposition of more and longer prison sentences since 1993 has had such a deterrent and/or incapacitative effect that there have been significant falls in the numbers of offences being committed. Yet since this decline has also been seen in some other countries (such as France, Germany and Finland) which have not pursued repressive policies, there can be no simple inference from increasing prison sentences to decreasing crime rates, as the recent Halliday Report recognised.[123] Nonetheless, the trends have made some government ministers more confident in calling for repressive measures, and it is in that context that the arguments in favour of recognising human rights must be pressed.

(ii) Two approaches to criminal process values

In part D of this lecture some 10 rights in criminal procedure were described. Justifications were offered for recognising each of them, and then some critical perspectives were discussed. One purpose of this was to show that these rights, no matter how fundamental they may be claimed to be, might be open to dispute and negotiation. Taking all those critical remarks together might enable us to describe an alternative approach to criminal process values that gives greater priority to "public interest" considerations.

On the one hand, we might sketch a rights-based approach which would respect the right to be presumed innocent until proved guilty, the privilege against self-incrimination, the right of silence, the right to legal aid and assistance, the right to be brought promptly before a court, the right to release pending trial, the right to disclosure of documents, the right to confrontation of witnesses, the right to be tried on evidence not obtained by the violation of fundamental rights, and the right not to be placed in double jeopardy. This approach gives a clear priority to the rights of suspects and defendants in the criminal process. If there is a conflict with the rights of another individual, such as the rights of a witness or victim, that conflict needs to be negotiated sympathetically but with an insistence on preserving the essence of each of the rights involved, recalling the discussion of victims' rights in part C(iii) above. The importance of preserving a defendant's right is particularly strong where respect for the right conflicts with some allegedly urgent "public interest" consideration, but the Strasbourg Court has not insisted on such stringent requirements when allowing exceptions to the right to release pending trial and, particularly, the right to be presumed innocent. Other aspects of the Strasbourg jurisprudence will be discussed in greater depth in the second lecture.

On the other hand, we might sketch an alternative approach. Its essential feature is a willingness to recognise a clear preference for "public interest" considerations when deciding on the entitlements of a suspect or defendant. It would not necessarily deny the right to be presumed innocent, but would argue that this right must give way where there are strong "public interest" considerations flowing against it. It might recognise the privilege against self-incrimination and the right of silence, but would expect them to give way in the face of the need to prevent and detect serious crimes. It would probably take a more restrictive view of the right to legal assistance. It would regard the right to be brought promptly before the court as important, but not so important that exceptions should not be made where the authorities are investigating a really serious offence. It would tip the scales more strongly in favour of public safety and the protection of (potential) victims' rights when deciding on the extent of the right to release pending trial, and would argue for the greater use of pre-trial detention in the public interest. It would give great weight to the needs of law enforcement agencies when determining the proper extent of disclosure of documents, and when deciding whether a trial might proceed on the basis of written statements and without confrontation of certain witnesses. It would regard the question of obtaining evidence by a violation of rights as entirely separate from the fairness of the subsequent trial, and it would fully support the exceptions already incorporated in the right not to be placed in double jeopardy.

The credentials of this sceptical approach would immediately be challenged by supporters of a rights-based approach. This is because the sceptics would wish to claim that they recognise rights, whereas the counter-argument is that anyone who accepts that so-called rights can be overridden routinely by public interest considerations is guilty of self-contradiction. This is the argument, examined in detail in the second lecture, that rights are essentially claims against the majority, and that therefore they cannot be "rights" if they are vulnerable to simple subordination to public interest claims. The sceptics' argument would be that rights need to be balanced against the public interest, that the public interest should be accorded priority whenever it is strong and clear, and that this does not extinguish rights but acknowledges that they have an important place. Supporters of this view might also contend that few advocates of a rights-based approach are able to sustain their position without making some concessions to "public interest" arguments, in which case the whole debate concerns questions of degree. To an extent that may be true, but there are other fundamental issues to be discussed before the matter can be concluded. In particular, key concepts such as "rights", "public interest", "public safety" and "serious crime" need to be explored further.

In the end, although refinement of the key concepts will help to clarify the argument, it will be necessary to take a view and to express a preference for the sort of society in which one wants to live. To go back to the practical example with which we began, those preferences may usefully be assessed by thinking of how we would wish the police and the courts to deal with members of our family or friends who found themselves suspected of crime. What safeguards would we expect, and what rights would we claim, in that situation? So far as the mass media are concerned, the loudest preferences expressed in recent years have been in favour of penal repression, with more prison sentences, longer sentences, and indeed mandatory sentences for some types of case.[124] Those preferences have often spilled over into criminal procedure, with the curtailment of the right of silence, reform of the disclosure system and now proposals to make details of a defendant's criminal record available to courts. This is the political and legal context into which the Human Rights Act was projected, so soon after the election of a new government in 1997, and evidently without much realisation of the tensions with the prevailing direction of criminal justice policies. The rights in the European Convention now have a special claim on our attention, not only as a kind of higher law for Europe but also because they have been infused into our domestic law. Those rights were drafted over 50 years ago, and the Court has developed them in certain directions (and not in other directions). In the next lecture we will consider the thrust of some of the Strasbourg jurisprudence; we should also have in mind the deeper normative question, which is whether there are other claims that we should recognise as no less fundamental than those enumerated in the Convention. Considering both the jurisprudence of the Court and the strength of other claims in the context of contemporary European social and political circumstances, we are likely to find that there is much room for argument. Francesca Klug has claimed that "the concept of inalienable rights is aimed precisely at distinguishing those rights which are essential for the furtherance of human dignity from those which are not."[125] No claim has been made here about the inalienability of rights, but we have seen growing evidence that drawing the line to which Klug refers is both a contentious and a context-based enterprise.

---

[1] *e.g.* Home Office, *The War against Crime in England and Wales* (1964).

[2] For discussion of the two last-mentioned developments, see A. Ashworth, "The Decline of English Sentencing and other Stories", in M. Tonry and R. Frase (eds), *Sentencing and Sanctions in Western Countries* (Oxford U.P., 2001).

[3] The bulk of the discussion of particular rights concerned freedom of expression and freedom of religion, as s. 12 and 13 of the Human Rights Act 1998 demonstrate.

[4] *cf.* P. Hillyard, "The Normalization of Special Powers: from Northern Ireland to Britain", in N. Lacey (ed), *A Reader on Criminal Justice* (Oxford U.P., 1994).

[5] D. Kennedy, "The International Human Rights Movement: Part of the Problem?" [2001] E.H.R.L.R. 245, p. 246.

[6] Although such rights were the subject of special mention by the then Home Secretary, Jack Straw, during debates on the Bill: "the Bill not only concerns the rights of individuals in a narrow sense . . . . For example, those who are

charged with criminal offences have rights and we must recognise and protect those rights . . ." H.C.Deb., vol. 317, col. 1360.

[7] Sir T. Bingham, "The European Convention on Human Rights—Time to Incorporate" (1993) 109 L.Q.R. 390, p. 392.

[8] [2001] 2 W.L.R. 817.

[9] H.C. Deb., vol. 317, col. 1358.

[10] Foreword to J. Wadham and H. Mountfield, *Blackstone's Guide to the Human Rights Act 1998* (Blackstone, 1999).

[11] H.C. Deb., vol. 307, col. 769.

[12] J. Bentham, *Rationale of Judicial Evidence* (1827); for an accessible summary, see W.L. Twining, *Theories of Evidence: Bentham and Wigmore* (Weidenfeld and Nicolson, 1985), Chap. 2.

[13] S. Lloyd-Bostock, "The Effects on Juries of Hearing about the Defendant's Previous Criminal Record: a Simulation Study" [2000] Crim.L.R. 734.

[14] Lord Justice Auld, *Review of the Criminal Courts of England and Wales* (The Stationery Office, 2001), has made recommendations both for the introduction of a new form of intermediate tribunal, consisting of a district judge and two lay magistrates, and for the abandonment of many longstanding rules of evidence in favour of a more free system of proof.

[15] See Chap. 4 of M. Redmayne, *Expert Evidence and Criminal Justice* (Oxford U.P., 2001), on the problems of presenting statistical evidence to juries.

[16] Compare, *e.g. Landy* (1995) 16 Cr.App.R. (S) 908, p. 910 ("the circumstances in which you were arrested, namely, at the wheel of a car, albeit a car upside down, your conviction for this offence was inevitable"), with decisions such as *Martin* (1989) 88 Cr.App.R. 343 and *Conway* (1988) 88 Cr.App.R. 159.

[17] On this, see Royal Commission on Criminal Justice, *Report* (1993), p.57.

[18] See Redmayne, *Expert Evidence and Criminal Justice* (Oxford U.P., 2001).

[19] For elaboration, see A. Sanders and R. Young, *Criminal Justice* (2nd ed., Butterworths, 2000), pp. 280–282.

[20] In the leading case of *Doorson v. Netherlands*, discussed in part D8 below, the Strasbourg Court recognised that respect for the rights of a witness may lead to some curtailment of a defendant's right.

[21] See, for example, JUSTICE, *Victims in Criminal Justice* (1998).

[22] *e.g.* A. Ashworth, "Victim Impact Statements and Sentencing" [1993] Crim.L.R. 498; A. Ashworth, "Victims' Rights, Defendants' Rights and Criminal procedure", in A. Crawford and J. Goodey (eds), *Integrating a Victim Perspective within Criminal Justice* (Ashgate, 2000).

[23] See T. Tyler, *Why People Obey the Law* (Yale U.P., 1990), and the detailed analysis of his work in D.J. Galligan, *Due Process and Fair Procedures* (Oxford U.P., 1996), p. 91ff.

[24] www.homeoffice.gov.uk

[25] *The Times*, October 19, 2001.

[26] See the Commission's ruling in *C.C. v. United Kingdom* [1999] Crim.L.R. 228.

[27] The leading decision in English law is *Woolmington v. D.P.P.* [1935] A.C. 462, and the leading Strasbourg decision is *Salabiaku v. France* (1988) 13 E.H.R.R. 379.

[28] *Winship* (1970) 397 U.S. 358, p. 364; the first part of the quotation seems to imply that the government adjudges people guilty, whereas the task referred to is surely the prosecution, before an independent and impartial tribunal, of people who have been charged.

[29] R.A. Duff, *Trials and Punishments* (Cambridge U.P., 1986), p. 109.

[30] *cf.* P. Roberts, "Taking the Burden of Proof Seriously" [1995] Crim.L.R. 783.

[31] 397 U.S. 358 (1970), p. 363.

[32] R.M. Dworkin, "Principle, Policy and Procedure", in C. Tapper (ed.), *Crime, Proof and Punishment* (Oxford U.P., 1981), discussed by Ashworth, *The Criminal*

Process (2nd ed., Oxford U.P., 1998), pp. 50–52; see also, *e.g.* R. Friedman, "Anchors and Flotsam: is Evidence Law adrift?" (1998) 107 Yale L.J. 1921, at p. 1942.

33 Criminal Law Revision Committee, 11th Report, *Evidence (General)* (1972), para. 140, adopted in *Lambert* [2001] 3 W.L.R. 206.

34 *per* Dickson C.J.C. in *Whyte* (1988) 51 D.L.R. 4th 481.

35 Section 101 of the Magistrates' Courts Act 1980 has been interpreted as requiring this.

36 A. Ashworth and M. Blake, "The Presumption of Innocence in English Criminal Law" [1996] Crim.L.R. 306.

37 *e.g.* in the Public Order Act 1986: see [1987] Crim.L.R. 153–155.

38 *cf. R v. Kebilene, ex p. D.P.P.* [2000] 2 A.C. 326, and *Lambert* [2001] 3 W.L.R. 206; two relevant legislative provisions, imposing only evidential burdens on the defence when persuasive burdens might have been expected, are found in s. 118(2) of the Terrorism Act 2000 and s.53 of the Regulation of Investigatory Powers Act 2000.

39 The leading decision on Article 6(2), *Salabiaku v. France* (1988) 13 E.H.R.R. 379, does not contain persuasive reasoning, and in *Phillips v. U.K.* [2001] Crim.L.R. 817, the Court did not improve upon this.

40 [2001] 3 W.L.R. 206.

41 The process has begun: see, *e.g. Carass, The Times,* January 21, 2002, reinterpreting s. 206 of the Insolvency Act 1986 so as to impose only an evidential burden on the defence. For other possibilities, see, *e.g. Philcox v. Carberry* [1960] Crim.L.R. 563 on the offence of driving a vehicle without valid motor insurance; *cf.* the "essential elements" test propounded by Lord Woolf in *Lee Kwong-kut v. R.* [1993] A.C. 951, with which the ruling in *Philcox* and several other statutory provisions are inconsistent.

42 For a learned discussion, see P. Mirfield, *Silence, Confessions and Improperly Obtained Evidence* (Oxford U.P., 1997), esp. pp. 13–18.

43 See the recent review by S. Sedley, "Wringing out the Fault: Self-Incrimination in the 21st Century" (2001) 52 N.I.L.Q. 107.

44 For the first clear statement of this rationale, see *John Murray v. U.K.* (1996) 22 E.H.R.R. 29, para. 45.

45 *Saunders v. U.K.* (1997) 23 E.H.R.R. 313, para. 68.

46 *IJL, GMR and AKP v. U.K.* (2001) 33 E.H.R.R. 225, para. 100.

47 (2001) 33 E.H.R.R. 264.

48 *Funke v. France* (1993) 16 E.H.R.R. 297.

49 In the United States the Supreme Court has stopped short of including within the privilege most requirements to produce documents: see *Fisher v. U.S.* 425 U.S. 391 (1976).

50 See also *J.B. v. Switzerland* [2001] Crim.L.R. 748, holding that the imposition of "disciplinary fines" under tax legislation for failure to give information about the source of certain income breached the privilege against self-incrimination, because the sums involved were "not inconsiderable" and therefore exerted improper compulsion.

51 (1997) 23 E.H.R.R. 313.

52 *ibid.,* para. 69.

53 In decisions such as *Schmerber v. California* 384 U.S. 757 (1996) and *U.S. v. Hubbell* 120 S. Ct. 2037 (2000).

54 For different shades of this rationale, see *e.g.* P. Arenella, "*Schmerber* and the Privilege against Self-Incrimination: a Re-Appraisal" (1982) 20 Amer.Crim.L.R. 31, D.J. Galligan, "The Right to Silence Reconsidered", [1988] C.L.P. 80.

55 *cf.* K. Greenawalt, "Silence as a Moral and Constitutional Right" (1981) 23 *William & Mary L.R.* 15 with D. Dolinko, "Is there a Rationale for the Privilege against Self-Incrimination?" (1986) 33 U.C.L.A. Law Rev. 1063.

[56] See Sedley (above, n. 43), p. 117.

[57] W. Stuntz, "Self-Incrimination and Excuse" (1988) 88 Columbia L.R. 1227.

[58] D.J. Seidmann and A. Stein, "The Right to Silence helps the Innocent: a game-theoretical analysis of the Fifth Amendment privilege" (2000) 114 Harvard L.R. 431.

[59] *ibid.*, pp. 475–480.

[60] *ibid.*, pp. 438–439.

[61] I. Dennis, *The Law of Evidence* (1999), p. 155.

[62] Above, n. 46; it also runs counter to the decisions set out in part 2 of lecture 2, below.

[63] s. 35 of the Criminal Justice and Public Order Act 1994, discussed by I. Dennis, *The Law of Evidence* (Sweet & Maxwell, 1999), pp. 406–413.

[64] For a good summary of the research evidence on police questioning, see A. Sanders and R. Young, *Criminal Justice* (2nd ed., Butterworths, 2000), Chap. 5.

[65] The reverse of this argument suggests that adverse inference might be more justifiable in investigations that are not conducted by the police and where the person questioned is highly likely to be legally advised, such as fraud investigations: see Royal Commission on Criminal Justice, *Report* (1993), Chap. 4, para. 30.

[66] Royal Commission on Criminal Justice, *Report* (1993), p. 57.

[67] *ibid.*, pp. 54–55.

[68] *Averill v. U.K.* (2000) 31 E.H.R.R. 839, para. 47.

[69] *Condron v. U.K.* (2000) 31 E.H.R.R. 1, para. 57.

[70] *John Murray v. U.K.* (1996) 22 E.H.R.R. 29, at para. 47.

[71] This tends to support the substance, but not all the details, of ss. 36 and 37 of the Criminal Justice and Public Order Act 1994.

[72] See, *e.g.* Northern Ireland Human Rights Commission, *Making a Bill of Rights for Northern Ireland* (2001), p. 48.

[73] For discussion, see A. Sanders and R. Young, *Criminal Justice* (2nd ed., Butterworths, 2000), pp. 285–296.

[74] See n. 66–67 above.

[75] *John Murray v. U.K.* (1996) 22 E.H.R.R. 29, para. 66, which relates the need for access to a lawyer at the early stages of police questioning to the possibility of adverse inferences from failure to answer.

[76] In his survey, Pradel lists Belgium, Croatia, France, Germany, Greece, Netherlands and Sweden as disallowing lawyers during police questioning. English law, in the Police and Criminal Evidence Act 1984, goes beyond the minimum, as also does Polish law. See J. Pradel, "The Criminal Justice Systems Facing the Challenge of Organised Crime" (1988) 69 *Revue Internationale de Droit Pénal* 673, p. 677.

[77] *cf. John Murray v. U.K., ibid.* where the justifications in the Northern Ireland (Emergency Provisions) Act 1987 for withholding access to a lawyer were discussed: the Court held that the right "may be subject to restrictions for good cause" (para. 62). However, in *Brennan v. U.K.* [2002] Crim.L.R. 214 the Court found that the right had been breached, on the ground that there was no "good cause" for insisting that the accused could only communicate with his lawyer under the supervision of a police officer. The Court held that this must have prevented the applicant from speaking frankly about his case.

[78] Ashworth, *The Criminal Process*, Chap. 9.

[79] *ibid.* pp. 77–78.

[80] *Brogan v. U.K.* (1989) 11 E.H.R.R. 117, para. 58.

[81] *e.g. Brogan v. U.K.,* above, and *Brincat v. Italy* (1993) 16 E.H.R.R. 591.

[82] For a review of the law and the research, see A. Sanders and R. Young, *Criminal Justice* (2nd ed., Butterworths, 2000), pp. 201–214.

[83] See, *e.g. R. v. Commissioner of Police for the Metropolis, ex p. M and LaRose* [2002] Crim.L.R. 213.

[84] (1989) 11 E.H.R.R. 117.

[85] The text of the derogation is reproduced in Schedule 2 to the Human Rights Act 1998.

[86] See H. Fenwick, *Civil Rights: New Labour, Freedom and the Human Rights Act* (Longman, 2000), pp. 76–80.

[87] See, *e.g.* D. Pannick, *The Times*, December 4, 2001.

[88] See part C(iii) above.

[89] *e.g. O'Hara v. Chief Constable of the Royal Ulster Constabulary* [1997] 1 All E.R. 129, and *O'Hara v. U.K.*, judgment of October 16, 2001.

[90] A. Sanders & R. Young, *Criminal Justice* (2nd ed., Butterworths, 2000), pp. 141–179.

[91] For a brief discussion of those cases, see A. Ashworth, *The Criminal Process* (2nd ed., Oxford U.P., 1998), Chap. 1.

[92] This connection with Article 6(3)(b) was made by the Commission in the early decision in *Jespers v. Belgium* (1981) 27 D.R. 61, para. 58.

[93] *Edwards v. U.K.* (1992) 15 E.H.R.R. 417, para. 36; *Rowe and Davis v. U.K.* (2000) 30 E.H.R.R. 1, para. 60.

[94] *ibid.*, para. 61. Note that the reasons for the grounds of exception differ in their nature: a conflict between individual rights may raise different considerations from a clash between an individual right and the public interest.

[95] Attorney General, *Disclosure of Information in Criminal Proceedings* (2000), para. 3.

[96] See the report of the Crown Prosecution Service Inspectorate, *Thematic Review of the Disclosure of Unused Material* (2000).

[97] See, *e.g.* J. McEwan, *Evidence and the Adversary Process* (2nd ed., Hart, 1998), pp. 106–115.

[98] See, *e.g. Rowe and Davis v. U.K.*, above, n. 93.

[99] *Van Mechelen v. Netherlands* (1997) 25 E.H.R.R. 647, para. 54.

[100] *Trivedi v. U.K.* (1997) 89A D.R. 136.

[101] For a recent example, see *Luca v. Italy* [2001] Crim.L.R. 747; *cf. Trivedi* (last note).

[102] See Council of Europe, *Intimidation of Witnesses and the Rights of the Defence*, Recommendation R (97) 13; N.R. Fyfe, *Protecting Intimidated Witnesses* (Ashgate, 2001).

[103] *Austria v. Italy* 2 Dig. 722 (Commission); in English law the provision requiring the exclusion of a confession obtained by "oppression" in s.76(1) of the Police and Criminal Evidence Act 1984 may be said to have the same effect. However, what about real evidence discovered in consequence of a confession obtained by oppression?

[104] See, *e.g. Teixeira de Castro v. Portugal* (1999) 28 E.H.R.R. 101, and the broadly similar decision of the House of Lords in *Looseley* [2001] UKHL 53. The Strasbourg Court applied *Khan* in *P.G. and J.H. v. U.K.* (judgment of September 25, 2001), but see the challenging dissent by Judge Tulkens.

[105] *Khan v. U.K.* (2001) 31 E.H.R.R. 45, supporting the views of the House of Lords in *Khan* [1997] AC 558; *cf.* now *Sargent* [2001] UKHL 54.

[106] An argument along similar lines was developed by Lord Woolf C.J. in *Attorney General's Reference (No. 2 of 2001)* [2001] EWCA Crim. 1568, when he held that a breach of the guarantee of trial within a reasonable time might suitably be dealt with, not by staying the prosecution or quashing the conviction, but by means of mitigation of sentence or financial compensation.

[107] *per* Black J. in *Green v. U.S.* 355 U.S. 184 (1957), pp. 187–188.

[108] For a discussion of recent official proposals, and their foundations, see I. Dennis, "Rethinking Double Jeopardy: Justice and Finality in Criminal Process" [2000] Crim.L.R. 933.

[109] Protocol 7 to the Convention, Article 4.2.

[110] Criminal Appeal Act 1995.

[111] Law Com. No. 267, *Double Jeopardy and Prosecution Appeals* (2001).

[112] For a discussion of the value of statistics of recorded crimes, see M. Maguire, "Crime Statistics, Patterns and Trends", in M. Maguire, R. Morgan and R. Reiner (eds), *Oxford Handbook of Criminology* (2nd ed., Oxford U.P., 1997).

[113] *Criminal Statistics 2000.*

[114] These figures includes all firearms (including air weapons), but exclude cases where the offence was criminal damage.

[115] All figures are taken from *Criminal Statistics, England and Wales 1999.*

[116] *ibid.*, Table 4.4.

[117] J. Harris and S. Grace, *A question of evidence? Investigating and prosecuting rape in the 1990s* (Home Office Research Study 196), Table 2.1.

[118] See, *e.g.* M. Hough, *Anxiety about crime: findings from the 1994 British Crime Survey* (Home Office Research Study 147).

[119] Home Office, *Digest 4: Information on the Criminal Justice System in England and Wales* (1999), p. 29.

[120] *ibid.*, where it is estimated that some 16 per cent of woundings resulted in a caution or conviction.

[121] See A. von Hirsch, A.E. Bottoms, E. Burney and P.-O. Wikstrom, *Criminal Deterrence and Sentence Severity* (Hart, 1999).

[122] *Digest 4* (above, n. 119), p. 29.

[123] Home Office, *Making Punishments Work*, Report of a Review of the Sentencing Framework for England and Wales (2001), Appendix 6.

[124] *e.g.* D. Garland, *The Culture of Control* (Oxford U.P., 2001), Chap. 5; J. Pratt, "The Return of the Wheelbarrow Man: Or, the Arrival of Postmodern Penality?" (2000) 40 B.J.Crim. 127, pp. 133–134.

[125] F. Klug, *Values for a Godless Age* (Penguin, 2000), p. 197.

2. Evaluating the Strasbourg and British approaches

In the first lecture I took stock of two strong streams in English public policy. First, I discussed the claims of various individual rights to be recognised as standards of justice and fairness. These were put forward as instrumental rights, that is, not as something inherent which stems from the nature of human existence but rather as something essential in order to avoid one kind of society and to facilitate a range of other kinds of society. By looking briefly at the justifications for 10 rights connected with the criminal process, and at what might happen in the absence of recognition of such rights, a case was made for regarding them as worthy of protection. It would have been possible to short-circuit the argument simply by declaring that nine of the rights are recognised by the European Convention on Human Rights and therefore ought to be respected because the United Kingdom has signed up to the Convention; but one of the purposes of these lectures is to generate wider discussion of the foundations for these rights, a discussion that never took place before or at the time of the enactment of the Human Rights Act. Secondly, the discussion shifted to the high incidence of crime, and fear of crime, in contemporary society. Whilst the number of recorded homicides seems to be relatively stable in England and Wales, this country shares with many others an anxiety about the apparent rise of organised crime, drug trafficking, serious fraud, child sex abuse—and, of course, terrorism. Law enforcement agencies lobby for greater powers to combat these activities, usually drawing a sympathetic response from substantial sections of the press and politicians, and this accounts for the vigorous stream of tough policies.

A collision is then likely to take place. The wider powers proposed for law enforcement agencies may clash with some of the procedural rights which, we have agreed, ought to be respected. What should happen next? In this second lecture I want chiefly to explore the way in which the European Court of

51

Human Rights in Strasbourg has handled this question, which (not surprisingly) has come before it several times. I then consider briefly some of the responses of the British courts during the first year of the Human Rights Act, again focusing on the criminal process rights in Articles 5 and 6 rather than on the Convention in general. I then examine the implications of "public interest" and "public safety" arguments for the very concept of rights, and consider some critical attacks on the notion of human rights. The starting point is practice under the Convention.

A. THE STRASBOURG COURT: THE EARLY YEARS

One of the first cases in which the European Court of Human Rights had to deal with a public interest argument grounded in the seriousness of the crimes concerned was *Klass v. Germany* in 1978.[1] German law established a procedure whereby the mail and telephone calls of certain individuals could be intercepted if the relevant Minister found that the necessary criteria for interception were fulfilled, and the surveillance was overseen by a judicial officer. The question for the Court was whether this system infringed the Article 8 rights of the applicants: they claimed that their right to respect for their private life was violated by the surveillance, and that there was insufficient justification for the interference with their rights. They claimed, in other words, that the conditions in Article 8, paragraph 2, were not satisfied:

> There shall be no interference by a public authority with the exercise of [the right to respect for private life] except such as is in accordance with the law and is necessary in a democratic society in the interests of national security, public safety or the economic well-being of the country, for the prevention of disorder or crime, for the protection of health or morals, or for the protection of the rights and freedoms of others.

The Government's argument to the Court was that the threats from terrorism, espionage and other forms of subversion were such that powers of this kind were essential in a democratic society. The Court accepted this submission, holding that:

> the existence of some legislation granting powers of secret surveillance over the mail, post and telecommunications is, under

exceptional conditions, necessary in a democratic society in the interests of national security and/or for the prevention of disorder or crime.[2]

More significant in the present context, however, is the restrictive approach that the Court adopted in the rest of its judgment. A sceptical view of the second paragraph of Article 8, quoted above, would be that its list of possible heads of justification is capable of legitimising almost any interference with a person's Article 8 rights, but in the very next paragraph of its judgment, this statement is to be found:

> The Court, being aware of the danger such a law poses of undermining or even destroying democracy on the ground of defending it, affirms that the Contracting States may not, in the name of the struggle against espionage and terrorism, adopt whatever measures they deem appropriate.[3]

In this vein the Court went on to insist that the system should ensure that any interference with Article 8 rights was kept to a minimum, and that there should be independent authorisation procedures. Indeed, the Court recognised that surveillance is "a field where abuse is potentially so easy in individual cases and could have such harmful consequences for democratic society as a whole," raising the spectre of secret police and uncontrolled State surveillance. The Court therefore emphasised the importance of an independent body which could "exercise an effective and continuous control", adding that "it is in principle desirable to entrust supervisory control to a judge."[4] In the end the Court held that the German legislation was compatible with Article 8, and so the application failed. This is an outcome that should put readers on their guard, because it is not unknown for courts to declaim resounding principles and then to apply them in a way that weakens their practical application. We must therefore examine some of the subsequent decisions in order to determine whether the *Klass* judgment is to be interpreted at face value.

Two cases decided about 10 years later explore the relationship between Article 5 and the public interest argument in favour of special powers to deal with suspected terrorists. In *Brogan v. United Kingdom*[5] the four applicants had been detained for periods between four and nearly seven days without being brought before a court, and they alleged that this violated their Article 5 rights. The Court found, by a majority, that in all four cases there had been a breach of the requirement in Article 5(3) that a detained person be brought before a court "promptly". The Court recognised that in the context of terrorism it may be justifiable to detain people for longer without judicial review, but held that this must be "subject to the existence of adequate safeguards." Thus to interpret the Convention as allowing detention for four days or longer in terrorist cases:

> would import into Article 5(3) a serious weakening of the procedural guarantee to the detriment of the individual and would entail consequences impairing the very essence of the right protected by this provision . . . The undoubted fact that the arrest and detention of the applicants were inspired by the legitimate aim of protecting the community as a whole from terrorism is not on its own sufficient to ensure compliance with the specific requirements of Article 5(3).[6]

A similar approach is seen in *Fox, Campbell and Hartley v. United Kingdom*,[7] a decision of 1990 arising from the arrest and detention of the applicants under the Prevention of Terrorism Act 1978. The argument for the applicants was that the Act provided a power for a police officer to arrest "any person whom he suspects of being a terrorist", and that this failed to comply with the requirements of Article 5(1)(c), which refer to "lawful arrest . . . on reasonable suspicion of having committed an offence." The Court agreed with the Government's argument that "terrorist crime falls into a special category" since the risk of "loss of life and human suffering" may require the police to act on information from secret sources, but held that the requirement of reasonableness should still be applied, and insisted that:

> the exigencies of dealing with terrorist crime cannot justify stretching the notion of 'reasonableness' to the point where the essence of the safeguard secured by Article 5(1)(c) is impaired.[8]

The Court held that, even taking account of the need to protect confidential sources, the State must furnish "at least some facts or information capable of satisfying the Court that the arrested person was reasonably suspected of having committed the alleged offence." The only fact advanced in this case was that two of the three applicants had a previous conviction for a terrorist offence, and the Court held that this could not "form the sole basis of a suspicion justifying their arrest some seven years later."[9] The Court therefore found a violation of Article 5 on the basis that the State's justification for the arrest failed to meet the minimum standard of reasonable suspicion.

The principle of these decisions might appear to have been diluted by the decision in *Margaret Murray v. United Kingdom*,[10] where breaches of Article 5 (no reasonable suspicion for arrest) and Article 8 (suspect photographed without her permission) were alleged. On the facts the Court, differing from the majority of the Commission, found no violations of the Convention. What is noticeable is that the Court began by stating:

> The Court sees no reason to depart from the general approach it has adopted in previous cases of a similar nature. Accordingly, for the purposes of interpreting and applying the relevant provisions of the Convention, due account will be taken of the special nature of terrorist crime, the threat it poses to democratic society and the exigencies of dealing with it.[11]

This statement is followed by footnote references to the passages from *Brogan* and from *Fox, Campbell and Hartley* discussed above.[12] We have seen that those were cases in which the Court went on to find violations of the Convention, but it is instructive that the above passage was cited by Lord Hope in *Kebilene*[13] without reference to the earlier decisions, thereby giving the impression that the Court's general approach was to allow curtailment of rights in Article 5 and 6 where the prevention of terrorism was the goal. That does not square with the evidence presented here.

The significance of the decisions in *Brogan* and *Fox, Campbell and Hartley* is difficult to assess. They can certainly be read as confirming that any justifications which States may advance for more extensive powers against terrorists are likely to be dealt with robustly when one of the strong rights, such as those in Article 5, is in question. It is to be noted, however, that Article 15 of the Convention does allow States to derogate from Articles 5 and 6 in situations of "public emergency", and once this power has been exercised the scrutiny of anti-terrorist measures may be less exacting.[14] Moreover, the Court in *Brogan* did recognise that special considerations might apply to terrorist cases, and this qualification may be said to have laid the ground for subsequent decisions which have made certain concessions to the anti-terrorism argument.[15] Nonetheless, the *Brogan* and *Fox* decisions are also significant because in both cases the Court, having recognised the need for special terrorist laws, found a violation of Article 5.[16] This should be sufficient to dispose of the sceptical reading of the *Klass* decision under Article 8, which depicted the Court as using words which favoured rights but reaching an outcome which favoured the "public safety" argument. In the two Article 5 cases, the Court used words which recognised that the "public safety" argument should be accorded some force but reached an outcome which favoured rights.

B. PUBLIC SAFETY AND ARTICLE 6

I now turn to consider how similar arguments, based on public safety and the protection of the public, have fared in the context of Article 6. Although the decisions discussed so far have been concerned with anti-terrorist measures, the focus henceforth will be on other serious crimes such as drug trafficking, organised crime and serious fraud, where arguments for special powers and special treatment have also been pressed. Article 6 of the Convention establishes strong rights, like Article 5, and is not subject to a list of justifiable grounds for interference as found in the second paragraphs of Articles 8, 9, 10 and 11. The essence of Article 6 is the right to a fair trial, some features of which are elaborated in Article 6(1). Some six special rights for criminal cases are declared in paragraphs (2) and (3) of Article 6. These will be set out as we come across them.

In *Kostovski v. Netherlands*,[17] the domestic court had convicted the applicant of armed robbery on the basis of statements by two anonymous witnesses. Only one of them had appeared before an examining judge, and that appearance was in the absence of the applicant and his counsel. Article 6(3)(d) of the Convention declares that everyone charged with a criminal offence has the right of confrontation, that is:

> the right to examine or have examined witnesses against him and to obtain the attendance and examination of witnesses on his behalf under the same conditions as witnesses against him.

This has been interpreted to mean that the conditions under which a witness is examined must enable the trial court and the defendant, or at least his counsel, to observe the demeanour of the witness. "In principle, all the evidence must be produced in the presence of the accused at a public hearing with a view to adversarial argument."[18] Although this had not been ensured in *Kostovski*, the Government's argument was that in the struggle against organised crime it was necessary to take protective measures, and that the fear of reprisals justified maintaining the anonymity of the witnesses. The Court's reaction was that:

> the government's line of argument, whilst not without force, is not decisive. Although the growth in organised crime doubtless demands the introduction of appropriate measures, the government's submissions appear to the Court to lay insufficient weight on what the applicant's counsel described as 'the interests of everybody in a civilized society in a controllable and fair judicial procedure.' The right to a fair administration of justice holds so prominent a place in a democratic society that it cannot be sacrificed to expediency.[19]

The Court concluded that the restrictions on the rights of the defence in this case were such as to deprive the applicant of a fair trial, and a violation of Article 6 was found. The Court took the same approach in the similar case of *Windisch v. Austria*,[20] where a conviction had been based on the statements of two anonymous witnesses who were not heard by the trial court or examined in the presence of the applicant or the defence lawyers. Fear of reprisals, together with the need to retain the co-operation of the public in investigating crimes, were advanced as reasons for the restrictions on the defence in this case. The Court held that the right in Article 6(3)(d) could not be restricted to such an extent.

A similar approach was taken in *Saidi v. France*,[21] where the French Government had argued that reliance on the statements of two anonymous witnesses was justified because it was difficult to obtain the attendance of witnesses in drugs cases and reprisals against witnesses were always likely. Finding that the applicant's conviction was based solely on the statements of two people whom neither he nor his counsel had had the opportunity to examine, the Court held:

> The lack of any confrontation deprived him in certain respects of a fair trial. The Court is fully aware of the undeniable difficulties of the fight against drug-trafficking—in particular with regard to obtaining and producing evidence—and of the ravages caused to society by the drug problem, but such considerations cannot justify restricting to this extent the rights of the defence of 'everyone charged with a criminal offence.' In short, there has been a violation of Article 6(1) and (3)(d).[22]

It will be observed that the Court objected to restricting the rights of the defence "to this extent". This may be said to go against the argument being developed here, since it clearly implies that some restriction may be acceptable. But, as will be argued below, there is a significant difference between allowing limited restrictions on a right and holding that any restriction that can be said to be proportionate to public interest considerations is permissible. What is noticeable about the relevant Strasbourg decisions is that they emphasise that the essence of the right must be preserved, even where limited restrictions are allowed. Thus in *Doorson v. Netherlands*[23] the Court recognised that the security of witnesses against threats and reprisals must be safeguarded, that their anonymity was therefore justifiable, and that this would "present the defence with difficulties which criminal proceedings should not normally involve." The Court therefore insisted that it must be:

established that the handicaps under which the defence laboured were sufficiently counterbalanced by the procedures followed by the judicial authorities.[24]

In this case the "counter-balancing" procedures were that the anonymous witnesses were questioned by the judge in the presence of defence counsel, who had an opportunity to ask questions, and that defence counsel were able to challenge the statements of the anonymous witnesses and to cast doubt on the reliability of their evidence. Of course the defence were handicapped because they did not know the identity of the witnesses and could therefore not attack their character. The Court also thought it relevant that in this case there was other significant evidence of the applicants' guilt. It is particularly important to note that this decision was reasoned on the basis of a clash between the defendant's rights (to a fair trial under Article 6) and the rights of witnesses (to physical security under Article 5), and not on the basis of a conflict between the defendant's rights and a broader public interest in the suppression of serious crime. The Court saw itself as protecting the rights of particular witnesses.[25]

All the decisions on Article 6 considered so far have concerned the right of a defendant to confront witnesses against him or her, and the extent to which this can be restricted. A rather different issue under Article 6 is whether a defendant's privilege against self-incrimination can be restricted when there are said to be public policy reasons for doing so. One difference here is that the right of silence and the privilege against self-incrimination are rights that have been implied into Article 6. They are not expressly stated in the Convention, but are declared in other human rights documents such as the International Covenant on Civil and Political Rights (Article 14), and the Strasbourg Court has taken the view that they should be regarded as essential elements in the right to a fair trial. Thus the Court in *Saunders v. United Kingdom* held that:

> although not specifically mentioned in Article 6 of the Convention, the right to silence and the right not to incriminate oneself are generally recognised international standards which lie at the heart of the notion of a fair procedure under Article 6. Their rationale lies, *inter alia*, in the protection of the accused against improper compulsion by the authorities, thereby contributing to the avoidance of miscarriages of justice and to the fulfilment of the aims of Article 6. The right not to incriminate oneself, in particular, presupposes that the prosecution in a criminal case seek to prove their case against the accused without resort to evidence obtained through methods of

coercion or oppression in defiance of the will of the accused. In this sense the right is closely linked to the presumption of innocence contained in Article 6(2) of the Convention.[26]

It is important to assess this strong statement in its context. The application by Ernest Saunders was based on the fact that he answered certain questions put by inspectors from the Department of Trade and Industry under compulsory powers in the Companies Act 1985 which provided for possible imprisonment for failure to answer; and the answers to the questions were subsequently used as part of the prosecution case against him at a trial for fraud. His argument was that his statements had been obtained by compulsion and then used against him. The Government's reply to this, at the hearing before the European Commission on Human Rights, was that the privilege against self-incrimination should be treated differently from the rights expressly set out in Article 6. Because it is only a right implied into Article 6 by the Court, the Government contended, it must be subject to "implied limitations which comply with the requirements of not impairing the very essence of a fair hearing, serve a legitimate aim and are proportionate to the aim sought to be achieved."[27] The Government's view was that these requirements were satisfied: this was an allegation of serious fraud, the inspector's powers were necessary to detect fraud, the Court had power to exclude unfairly obtained evidence, the defendant was under no compulsion to give evidence himself, and so on. The Commission's response was firm:

> It cannot be compatible with the spirit of the Convention that varying degrees of fairness apply to different categories of accused in criminal trials. The right of silence, to the extent that it may be contained in the guarantees of Article 6, must apply as equally to alleged company fraudsters as to those accused of other types of fraud, rape, murder or terrorist offences. Further, there can be no legitimate aim in depriving someone of the guarantees necessary in securing a fair trial.[28]

When the case went on from the Commission to the Court in Strasbourg, the Government continued to press its argument that the individual's right should be restricted because of the "public interest in the honest conduct of companies and in the effective prosecution of those involved in complex corporate fraud." Two particular arguments were adduced in support of this position: first, that corporate fraud cases had different characteristics, because of the complex company structures and the difficulty of understanding documentation without explanations from the persons involved; and secondly, that the typical defendant in corporate fraud would have access to expert legal advice. The Court was no more impressed with these arguments than the Commission had been. Finding that it was unfair to the applicant to base the prosecution on statements extracted from him on pain of imprisonment, because that violated his privilege against self-incrimination, the Court stated:

> It does not accept the Government's argument that the complexity of corporate fraud and the vital public interest in the investigation of such fraud and the punishment of those responsible could justify such a marked departure as that which occurred in the present case from one of the basic principles of a fair procedure. Like the Commission, it considers that the general requirements of fairness contained in Article 6, including the right not to incriminate oneself, apply to criminal proceedings in respect of all types of criminal offences without distinction, from the most simple to the most complex.[29]

This emerges as a clear and significant decision. It does not matter that the right of silence and the privilege against self-incrimination are not stated expressly in Article 6. They are basic principles, and they should not give way in the face of unusually complex or unusually serious types of case. In its decisions on the drawing of adverse inferences from silence, the Court has recognised that there may be circumstances "which clearly call for an explanation" from the defendant,[30] but this relates to the factual circumstances in the case and not to the type or category of crime charged.

Lest it be thought that the *Saunders* decision rested more on a rejection of the proposition that the *complexity* of the type of case should lead to restrictions on the right not to incriminate oneself, reference should be made to a decision squarely on the relevance of the *seriousness* of the type of offence. In *Heaney and McGuinness v. Ireland*,[31] the applicants had been convicted and imprisoned for failing to give a full account of their movements and actions during a specified period, under a statute aimed at terrorism. They claimed that their privilege against self-incrimination, and therefore their right to a fair trial, had been violated. The Government's response was that the public interest in taking measures to combat terrorism and protect the safety of citizens justified this restriction on the privilege. The Court unanimously found in favour of the applicants, and dismissed the Government's argument thus:

> The Court accordingly finds that the security and public order concerns of the Government cannot justify a provision which

extinguishes the very essence of the applicant's right to silence and against self-incrimination guaranteed by Article 6(1) of the Convention.[32]

The pressure to allow incursions in terrorist cases into the strong rights declared by Articles 5 and 6 is considerable, but it is a pressure that the Strasbourg Court has generally resisted.

One final example of the Court's approach comes from a drug dealing case, where the seriousness of the offences and the difficulty of detecting them were again argued strongly by the Government. The case is *Teixeira de Castro v. Portugal*,[33] the allegation was that the applicant had been entrapped into committing the offence by undercover police officers, and the claim was that this violated his right to a fair trial. Two aspects of the Court's decision are notable in the present context. First, there is no reference in Article 6 to a right not to be entrapped into committing a crime, but the Court showed no reluctance to find that, where a person commits an offence as a result of police incitement, this deprives that person of the possibility of a fair trial. Secondly, the Court was again confronted with a government argument that special investigative measures are necessary in order to combat drug trafficking. Its response was as follows:

> The use of undercover agents must be restricted and safeguards put in place even in cases concerning the fight against drug-trafficking. While the rise in organised crime undoubtedly requires that appropriate measures be taken, the right to a fair administration of justice nevertheless holds such a prominent place that it cannot be sacrificed for the sake of expedience. The general requirements of fairness embodied in Article 6 apply to proceedings concerning all types of criminal offence, from the most straightforward to the most complex.[34]

This is an unambiguous affirmation of the point. It brooks no balancing of "the public interest" against the right to a fair trial, and it makes no provision for "proportionality" arguments to eat into a strong right. Such arguments have a place in relation to the qualified rights, such as those in Articles 8–11, but not where, as with Articles 5 and 6, the right is a strong and unqualified one. However, the *Teixeira* decision still stands virtually alone in the Strasbourg jurisprudence, and there were strongly argued dissenting judgments.[35] It is therefore too soon to suggest that this principle is a firmly established part of the right to a fair trial.

C. BRITISH COURTS AND THE "PUBLIC INTEREST"

It has been and remains the position that, where the Strasbourg Court hands down a decision adverse to the government of a Member State, that government is obliged (through the mechanism of the Committee of Ministers) to give effect to the decision. Since the implementation of the Human Rights Act 1998, British courts also have certain direct obligations to apply Convention rights: section 6 requires courts and other public authorities to act in conformity with Convention rights, section 3 requires courts to interpret legislation so far as is possible in a way that applies the Convention, and section 2 requires courts to take account of the decisions of the Strasbourg organs, notably the Court.

In the first year or so since the implementation of the 1998 Act on October 2, 2000, the courts of England and Wales have invoked "public interest" arguments with some frequency when dealing with Convention rights. The Act has been in force longer in Scotland: the courts there have been less strongly drawn to the use of "public interest" arguments to limit the effect of Convention rights, but we will see that the Privy Council has relied on "public interest" arguments to overturn the Scottish courts on more than one occasion. First, however, we must go back to the Strasbourg jurisprudence. The decisions discussed in sections A and B above have not been prominent in the reasoning of the English courts. Instead, their attention has focused on a different strand of authorities, not surprisingly those which recognise that certain rights can be "balanced" against the "public interest". We must consider two sets of those authorities briefly, before going on to describe the approach of the House of Lords and Privy Council.

(i) Scattered Strasbourg Authorities on "Balancing":

First, even though it has been accepted that the right to a fair trial should not be "balanced" against other goals, leading British judges have adopted the view that there is room for balancing when deciding whether the trial has been fair.[36] In adopting this approach, they have taken their cue from a small number of over-broad statements made by the Strasbourg Court,[37] and have paid little attention to the authorities set out in part B above. It is true, however, to say that there is one Strasbourg decision on Article 6 which does appear to favour broad balancing—*Salabiaku v. France*,[38] a decision which takes the unqualified wording of Article 6(2) on the presumption of innocence and accepts that legislatures may reverse the burden of proof "within reasonable limits which take into account the importance of what is at stake and maintain the rights of the defence." Nevertheless, the Strasbourg jurisprudence on Article 6(2) is under-developed, and (paradoxically, one might say) it is British judges, taking their cue from Commonwealth constitutional courts, who have sought to give greater sharpness to the presumption of innocence and to limit any exceptions.[39]

It is not true, however, to say that the kind of broad "balancing" permitted by the *Salabiaku* decision is the norm under Article 6. Lord Bingham was surely not right to suggest that the Strasbourg approach to Article 6(3)(d) is similar.[40] He cited *Kostovski v. Netherlands*,[41] one of a number of decisions discussed in part B above, which holds—contrary to Lord Bingham's implication—that paragraph (3)(d) "cannot be sacrificed to expediency" even when governments put forward weighty public interest arguments.[42] The Strasbourg Court has accepted that the right under Article 6(3)(d) may be curtailed in order to protect the rights of an intimidated witness, but it is important to note that this is only acceptable if absolutely necessary, if accompanied by compensating safeguards for the defence, and if the defendant was not convicted solely or mainly on the basis of evidence thereby admitted.[43] Reasoning of that kind is a far cry from the unstructured language of balancing and of the *Salabiaku* judgment.

Secondly, there is some authority for the proposition that, where the Strasbourg Court has implied a right into Article 6, so it can equally restrict that right by balancing it against "the public interest". Although, once again, the Strasbourg case law falls short of consistency, there is scattered support for this thesis. The right of access to a court has been implied into Article 6, notably for those held in custody, as an element in (or logically prior to) the right to a fair trial: in *Ashingdane v. United Kingdom* the Court, in a passage much cited by British judges,[44] held that the right of access to courts "is not absolute but may be subject to limitations," as to the scope of which Member States have a certain (but not elastic) margin of appreciation.[45] The right to disclosure, as part of the principle of equality of arms, has also been implied into Article 6 and has been recognised to be subject to limited exceptions for reasons "such as national security or the need to protect witnesses at risk of reprisals or keep secret police methods of investigation of crime."[46] However, on disclosure, the Court has followed *Doorson v. Netherlands* in laying down strict conditions under which exceptions would be allowed, and has not resorted to any broad "balancing" approach.[47]

The doctrine that limitations may be implied into Article 6 where the right itself has been implied into the right to a fair trial does have some support in the Strasbourg jurisprudence,[48] but there are at least two other considerations that should be placed alongside it. The first derives from the general structure of the Convention, and it is developed more fully in section D below. In brief, it insists that any argument to the effect that a right implied into Article 6 should be restricted out of deference to the "public interest" should be required to be at least as strong, and probably stronger, than a similar argument for justifying interference with one of the qualified rights such as those under Articles 8–11. The right to a fair trial and its constituent elements should surely be given greater weight, in such calculations, than the rights in Articles 8–11.[49] The second point is that the Strasbourg decisions refer frequently to one doctrine which has received scant mention in the British cases: that no restriction should be such as to "destroy the very essence of the right".[50] This doctrine places distinct limits on "public interest" balancing of the kind that some British judges have found attractive.[51] Thus, even in relation to the implied right of access to the courts (where the idea of implied limitations has found most support), the doctrine of the "essence of the right" has been maintained.[52] How should this be applied to cases on the privilege against self-incrimination, where the notion of balancing was adopted with enthusiasm in the Privy Council?

(ii) The British Courts and Self-Incrimination:

The right to silence and the privilege against self-incrimination have both been implied into Article 6, by the Strasbourg Court, as elements of the fundamental right to a fair trial.[53] The Judicial Committee of the Privy Council in *Brown v. Stott*[54] was particularly keen to establish that neither the right nor the privilege is absolute, and there is good authority to that effect. In *John Murray v. United Kingdom* the Court held that adverse inferences from silence might reasonably be drawn "in situations which clearly call for an explanation from him," so long as a conviction was not based "solely or mainly" on such inferences.[55] In *Saunders v. United Kingdom* the Court mentioned at least twice the possibility that an infringement of the privilege against self-incrimination might be justifiable,[56] although it did not elaborate on this.

Nevertheless, to accept that these rights are not absolute is not to concede that they may be "balanced away" by being compared with a general public interest and put in second place. This is what happened in *Brown v. Stott*: Lord Bingham held that section 172 of the Road Traffic Act 1988 provides for the putting "of a single, simple question" rather than the prolonged questioning found objectionable in *Saunders*, and the general public interest in upholding a regulatory scheme for drivers of motor vehicles meant that this power was not a "disproportionate legislative response to the problem of maintaining road safety."[57] This course of reasoning assumes that, in determining restrictions on implied rights in Article 6, it is legitimate to "balance the general interests of the community against the interests of the individual." This is a broad approach to "balancing" and proportionality, for which there is scant support in the Article 6 jurisprudence and which is inherently doubtful since it appears less demanding than the "necessary in a democratic society" criterion in Articles 8–11. It is certainly far more easily satisfied than the criteria in *Doorson v. Netherlands*, developed in relation to Article 6(3)(d) and applied to the principle of equality of arms.[58] It makes no reference to preserving the essence of the right and, if applied generally within Article 6, it could lead to the "balancing away" of various rights. Only the Strasbourg judgment in *Salabiaku v. France*, as we have already noted,[59] is flexible enough to support this approach.

Since *Brown v. Stott* was decided, the Strasbourg Court has handed down at least two decisions which insist on a much firmer line. In *Heaney and McGuinness v. Ireland*[60], as we saw in section B above, the Court held that the degree of compulsion arising from the (threat of a) prison sentence "destroyed the very essence of their privilege against self-incrimination and their right to remain silent."[61] Moreover, the Court gave explicit approval to its earlier decision in *Funke v. France*,[62] where it held that the privilege was violated when the sanction for non-production of documents was accumulating fines. Consistent with this last point is the subsequent decision in *J.B. v. Switzerland*,[63] where tax authorities had imposed disciplinary fines on the applicant for failure to furnish information required by statute. The Court held that the fines constituted "improper compulsion," and therefore that the privilege against self-incrimination had been violated.

The effect of these Strasbourg decisions is to call into serious question the general "balancing" approach that seems so intuitive for British judges,[64] as well as the specific reasoning of the Privy Council in *Brown v. Stott*. For the Strasbourg Court, it is

not simply a question of considering whether there is a significant public interest in compelling a person to speak: the Court's
dismissal of the Irish Government's "fight against terrorism"
argument in *Heaney and McGuinness* makes that clear.[65] Proportionate or not, the compulsion to speak destroyed the essence of
the right and rendered it ineffective. That case would surely not
have been decided differently if emphasis had been placed on
the fact that the applicants had been asked "a single, simple
question."[66] Moreover, compulsion arising from financial penalties may be sufficient to invoke the privilege, as the *Funke* and
J.B. decisions demonstrate, so the argument that section 172 of
the Road Traffic Act 1988 prescribes only modest penalties
should not, of itself, save it from incompatibility with Article 6.[67]

One particular distinction between the prevailing Strasbourg
and British approaches is that, although they share the view that
the rights in Articles 5 and 6 are not absolute, they differ as to
what this means. For the British judges, it is taken to indicate the
propriety of balancing the right against public interest considerations, and the reliance on a concept of proportionality as
broad as that applied in Articles 8–11. To the Strasbourg judges,
it is not usually treated as opening the way to a general
balancing exercise, and in the rare situations where the special
force of public interest considerations is recognised, it is taken to
require a three-way adjustment between the essence of the right
itself, the public interest considerations, and safeguards for the
suspect or defendant. This triangulated approach[68] was taken in
Doorson v. Netherlands,[69] for example, and we shall see in the
third lecture that the provision of safeguards is often taken to be
a significant indicator of an overall commitment to fairness.

None of this is to suggest that the approach of the Strasbourg
Court is unproblematic. The decisions discussed extensively in
section B above appear powerful when read alone, but it is not
clear how they would stand with decisions such as *Salabiaku v.
France, Ashingdane v. United Kingdom*, and the others mentioned
in part (i) of this section. The Court has never considered how
the "essence" doctrine applies to other rights implied into
Article 6, let alone how it applies to the *presumption* of innocence
in Article 6(2), so readily balanced away in *Salabiaku*.[70] Nor has
the Court considered in one judgment the various streams of
authority on silence and self-incrimination. The decision in *J.B.
v. Switzerland* fails to mention *Heaney and McGuinness v. Ireland*,
probably the most striking case. Both *Heaney and McGuinness*
and *Saunders* accept that the privilege against self-incrimination
is not absolute, but it has not yet emerged what the significance
of this qualification is. Both *Saunders* and *J.B.* insist that the

privilege does not attach to evidence "which has an existence independent of the accused's will", a category that includes blood or urine samples but not documents.[71] No rationale for these limitations on the privilege has been offered by the Court.[72]

(iii) The British Courts and Unreasonable Delay:

Article 6 of the Convention declares that "everyone is entitled to a fair and public hearing within a reasonable time." Where there has been such an unreasonable delay as to constitute a violation of Article 6, this indicates that the defendant did not receive a fair trial, and in principle the conviction should be quashed.[73] The Privy Council in *Darmalingum v. State*,[74] interpreting the Mauritius constitution which grants the right to a fair trial within a reasonable time, held that the only remedy which would vindicate this constitutional right was to quash the conviction. However, the Privy Council took a different view in *Flowers v. R.*,[75] holding that a similar provision in the constitution of Jamaica should be interpreted so as to give weight to the seriousness of the offences of violence with which Flowers had been charged. Thus it held that the right to trial within a reasonable time "must be balanced against the public interest in the attainment of justice", which weighs more heavily for serious crimes.

This balancing approach was embraced with enthusiasm by the Court of Appeal in *Attorney-General's Reference (No. 2 of 2001)*,[76] where Lord Woolf C.J. held, without referring to the recent Strasbourg decisions,[77] that:

> it is not only the defendant who is to be considered. The public are interested in whether or not defendants are tried for criminal offences they have committed [*sic*]. As is the case with many of the rights which are contained in the Convention, the courts are called upon to hold the balance between the rights of the individual and the rights of the public.[78]

This led the Court of Appeal to hold that a finding of unreasonable delay should not result inevitably in a stay of the prosecution or a quashing of the conviction (depending on the stage which the case has reached), and that courts should consider mitigation of sentence or even financial compensation as remedies in appropriate cases. The general approach of the Court of Appeal seems at odds with the Strasbourg decisions, which place greater emphasis on the importance of the right and do not "balance" it against public interest considerations.

(iv) The British Courts and the Right to Impartiality:

Brief reference may be made to the problems caused by prejudicial media coverage of criminal proceedings, and the effect this may have on the right to a fair hearing by an "independent and impartial tribunal." After Lord Hope had reviewed the Strasbourg case law[79] in *Montgomery and Coulter v. H.M. Advocate*,[80] he considered the Scots law requirement that the court should balance the interests of the defendant in having a fair trial against the public interest in ensuring that serious crime is prosecuted:

> The right of an accused to have a fair trial by an independent and impartial tribunal is unqualified. It is not to be subordinated to the public interest in the detection and suppression of crime . . . The only question to be addressed in terms of Article 6(1) of the Convention is the right of an accused to a fair trial. An assessment of the weight to be given to the public interest does not enter into the exercise.[81]

This is an important re-statement of the Strasbourg approach. It is reasoning of this kind which should have been adopted by the Court of Appeal when dealing with the right to trial within reasonable time, rather than the broad "balancing" of the public interest which Lord Woolf favoured.

(v) The British Courts and the Presumption of Innocence:

On the application of the presumption of innocence in Article 6(2) to reverse onus provisions, which place the burden on the defence in respect of certain elements, the two judicial systems are to be found on the opposite sides of the fence. Thus it is the Strasbourg Court that has accepted presumptions and other reverse onus provisions, so long as the legislation "confines them within reasonable limits which take into account the importance of what is at stake and maintain the rights of the defence"—a qualification applied with considerable breadth, since in *Salabiaku v. France*[82] a reverse onus provision was upheld for an offence carrying a maximum penalty of imprisonment. The House of Lords in *Lambert*,[83] on the other hand, held that in principle the burden of proof should remain on the prosecution, and that the mere fact that this might make it more difficult to prosecute drugs cases was not a sufficient reason for upholding a reverse onus interpretation.

Thus, in decisions on the presumption of innocence and the right to trial by an impartial tribunal, public interest arguments have not been allowed to prevail. In other fair trial cases, particularly where a right has been implied into Article 6, the British courts have "balanced" the right against public interest considerations and have allowed the right to be displaced. In doing so, they have drawn little distinction between proportionality under the qualified rights in Articles 8–11[84] and the position under Articles 5 and 6.

D. THE STRENGTH OF PUBLIC INTEREST ARGUMENTS

We have seen that the responses of the Strasbourg Court and the British courts to arguments based on the "public interest" or public safety have been somewhat different. The approach of the British courts has been variable, but predominantly in favour of allowing public interest arguments and proportionality judgments to overpower elements of the right to a fair trial. The Strasbourg response to public interest arguments in respect of rights under Article 5 or 6 has also been mixed, but predominantly in favour of resisting arguments that public interest considerations should be allowed to outweigh these strong rights. There has been a measure of recognition of public interest arguments in terrorism decisions such as *Brogan*,[85] but the result in that case and subsequent decisions such as *Heaney and McGuinness*[86] tell strongly against diluting rights. Limited concessions to public interest considerations have been allowed in two other implied rights,[87] but the unimpressive judgment on the presumption of innocence in *Salabiaku v. France* (see part C(i) above) stands virtually alone in allowing an express right to be balanced against public interest considerations, to the extent that its essence disappears.

In political theory there are several different approaches to the concept of the "public interest".[88] In practice, governments often start from a position in which there is great concern, domestically or even internationally, about crimes of a certain type. They decide to promote legislation to "tackle" the crime, which may sometimes have the effect of trampling on what ought to be fundamental rights. One obvious line of justification is to say that, whilst we recognise the good reasons for upholding individual rights in general, it is in the public interest to allow exceptions when the demands of public safety are particularly pressing. A different version of the same argument is to say that it is important to keep a balance between individual rights and public safety and that, although respect for fundamental rights should usually prevail, the balance may be tipped towards the protection of public safety when we are dealing with serious crimes which there is a strong public interest in tackling. Is there anything wrong with these kinds of justification?

(i) What is the "public interest"?

I suggest that there may be at least four difficulties with this approach. The first way in which the apparent "common sense" of this approach fails to sustain a convincing argument is its seductive but insubstantial use of the notion of "the public interest". The phrase itself assumes that there is a single public interest, "*the* public interest", whereas there might be a stronger case for arguing that there are "public interests" which may conflict with private interests. Even at that, however, it seems to be assumed that public interests lie only in the suppression of these serious types of crime: references to "public interests" are therefore one-dimensional, it being assumed that the maximum pursuit of public safety is the only worthwhile interest. This overlooks the interest of citizens in the preservation of fundamental rights. If we go back to the first lecture and recognise that it can equally be said to be in the public interest that basic rights are upheld, then to say that the suppression of serious crimes is in the public interest is not the knock-down argument that it is sometimes made to appear. At best, we have two conflicting public interests or, better, a conception of public interest which includes some goals which may come into conflict with one another. What we have to resolve is how to deal with that kind of conflict—which, of course, is where we started.

(ii) "Public interests", fundamental rights and democratic processes

A second way of attacking public interest arguments is to argue that they contradict the very notion of fundamental rights. By saying that someone has a fundamental right to do X, to have X, or not to be prevented from doing X, one is surely saying that this is a claim that cannot be overridden by a simple "public interest" argument. Now this is to enter controversial territory, and there are many erudite contributions to this debate which cannot even be reviewed here, let alone argued against. What I would hope to do is simply to establish, at a minimum level, that if one calls something a fundamental right, this implies that it is something that cannot be taken away merely by showing that a majority of people would be better off if it were not applied in a given situation. A basic right is therefore essentially a counter-majoritarian or anti-utilitarian concept. Why should anyone agree with this point? Some might answer that in this context it is inherent in the very idea of a fundamental right. This depends largely on the connotations of the adjective "fundamental" or "basic": these terms are being used here to signify a right that is not merely the correlative of some duty-imposing rule, but rather has a deeper significance which might be described in some countries (such as the United States or South Africa) as a constitutional right, or (as in the European Convention) as a "human right", or (as in both the European Convention and the European Union's Charter) as a "fundamental right". If a right of this kind is not a claim to be protected against the wishes (or interests) of a majority, then what is it? If it is something that can simply be taken away when a majority of people decide that this would benefit them more, is it a basic right? Surely if there is agreement that something should be recognised as a fundamental right, this must entail that it should be assigned some kind of preference or priority when political and legal policies are being determined; otherwise fundamental rights are not what they appear to be, and the label indicates merely an aspiration rather than an actuality.[89]

If human rights are by their nature counter-majoritarian, does this mean that they are essentially anti-democratic? In one sense the answer must be that they are: insofar as they are intended to, and do, operate as a restraint on legislation passed by normal democratic procedures, they tend to weaken the authority of the normal legislative processes and procedures established in a particular country. They may be thought to do so for a largely anti-democratic reason, too, insofar as they tend to protect certain interests of individuals or minorities which might otherwise be overwhelmed by a majority vote. This may be particularly appropriate to criminal procedure, where the interests in question are those of suspected (or sometimes convicted) criminals, for which there is unlikely to be a strong constituency of political support.

There are three general answers, and a fourth specific answer, to anyone who might argue that human rights undermine democratic processes. The first is that most domestic human rights bills and constitutions are themselves the product of the democratic process: the legislatures in Britain, Canada, Ireland, South Africa and many other countries have voted to introduce some kind of "rights" declaration that enables ordinary legislation to be treated in a different way by the courts, sometimes allowing the courts to declare legislative provisions unconstitutional and sometimes giving the courts some lesser (but still exceptional) power in relating to incompatible legislation. According to this answer, therefore, there is nothing anti-democratic about a constitutional entrenchment of rights which has itself been introduced by democratic processes, since its pedigree is no less democratic than that of the legislation impugned under the extraordinary powers.[90] Bills of rights are often examples of a process of (democratic) self-binding, which places above legislative voting practices a set of values which have been agreed to be fundamental to the way the government of a particular country should be conducted.[91] Indeed, one might add that certain rights, such as freedom of expression, are themselves essential elements in a system that wishes to describe itself as democratic.

A second possible answer is that recognition of human rights enhances democracy by increasing its legitimacy.[92] The force of this answer depends on the slippery idea of legitimacy, a splendid-sounding notion that begins to crumble when one asks whose view of the legitimacy of the system counts, and how one might reliably measure increases or reductions in legitimacy. One way of constructing a reasonably robust answer would be to relate legitimacy to compliance with international or regional standards: thus, for example, the United Kingdom is a signatory to the European Convention on Human Rights, and one of the criteria for allowing an emergent state to become a member of the Council of Europe is its preparedness to sign up to the Convention. But then there may be questions about the extent to which a particular country fails to respect the declared rights: would legitimacy be recognised even if a particular country was frequently found to be in violation of the Convention? No doubt this must be a question of degree, and it is a question in which people in the United Kingdom have a particular interest, since the United Kingdom has been one of the countries most frequently found to have violated the Convention. The Lord Chancellor expressly recognised this when introducing the Human Rights Bill:

> Our legal system has been unable to protect people in the 50 cases in which the European Court has found a violation of the Convention by the United Kingdom. That is more than any other country except Italy. The trend has been upwards. Over half the violations have been found since 1990.[93]

The upward trend has continued in the years since Lord Irvine's speech in 1997: the implementation of the Human Rights Act in autumn 2000 has not yet had an effect on the number of Strasbourg decisions adverse to the United Kingdom, and it remains to be seen how many applications to Strasbourg will be pursued now that British courts are able, indeed required, to give effect to Convention rights in their decisions. The judges' enthusiasm for "public interest" arguments, demonstrated in part C above, suggests that there may be further occasions on which applications to Strasbourg will succeed.

A third argument on the relation of human rights to democracy is to point out the obligation of states to ensure that fundamental rights are secured. Under the Convention each Member State has various "positive duties" to secure rights to its citizens by ensuring that the legal system provides adequate protection of the right to life, the right not to be subjected to inhuman and degrading treatment, the right to respect for one's private life, and so on.[94] At the level of political theory one may argue that one of the purposes of a state, or at least of a Western state that aspires to democracy, should be to protect basic rights. On this view, human rights are not to be regarded merely as restrictions on state action but rather as part of the rationale for having the State—an approach which runs through much of the German constitutional writing and the judgments of the Constitutional Court.[95] This conception of the relationship between the state and rights is not the common currency in the United Kingdom.

A fourth answer to the charge that human rights undermine democracy is specific to the approach adopted by the United Kingdom Parliament: that the structure of the Human Rights Act preserves a vital and final role for Parliament, in the sense that, even where the courts do make a "declaration of incompatibility" in respect of a particular statutory provision, Parliament has the opportunity but not the obligation to remedy the deficiency. As the Lord Chancellor argued, the Human Rights Act:

> will deliver a modern reconciliation of the inevitable tension between the democratic right of the majority to exercise political power and the democratic need of individuals and minorities to have their human rights secured.[96]

This shows recognition of the force of the argument that human rights may be regarded as anti-democratic, and responds to it constructively by institutionalising, under the 1998 Act, what Murray Hunt has called "a creative tension between the judiciary on the one hand and Parliament and the executive on the other."[97] It is too early to assess how this "creative tension" will work out, but there is some evidence of a tendency of judges to defer to the "democratic will" as expressed in legislation even when it is unlikely that Parliament considered the human rights implications of what it was doing.[98]

Human rights documents are thus intended to operate as an institutional check on the output of democratic processes, either from within that country (as where there is a constitutional or otherwise entrenched declaration of fundamental rights) or, and perhaps additionally, from outside that country (as under the European Convention on Human Rights). Whether these functions are described as anti-democratic depends on the relationship between the possible answers sketched above and the definition of democracy, a matter which will not be examined further in this context. What is abundantly clear, however, is that the practical interaction between majority interests and so-called rights gives way to considerable indeterminacy and contingency. It is one thing to argue that one cannot call something a right unless one is prepared to give it some kind of preference or protection in arguments about policies that should be pursued. It is quite another thing to specify how much preference and how much protection should be given.

(iii) Resolving conflicts between fundamental rights and the "public interest"

Few would contend that to recognise a right as fundamental is to assert that it must be protected in all situations. There may be some rights which are regarded as absolute, but there appears to be nothing inherent in the concept of a fundamental right which requires that it should only be applied to claims that are absolute and inviolable. On the other hand, inherent in the idea of basic rights there surely is the notion that simple majoritarian arguments should not be allowed to detract from their protection. Thus in developing his rights theory, Ronald Dworkin argues that there is no place for simply balancing a constitutional right against the public interest and then curtailing the right if there seems to be a social cost in maintaining it. He argues that to allow such reasoning would be to show that the original recognition of the right was a mere sham. However, he recognises that there might be circumstances in which it might be decided that, "although great social cost is warranted to protect the original right, this particular cost is not necessary." He outlines three grounds on which this might be an acceptable course of reasoning:

> First, the Government might show that the values protected by the original right are not really at stake in the marginal case, or at stake

only in some attenuated form. Second, it might show that if the right is defined to include the marginal case, then some competing right, in the strong sense described earlier, would be abridged. Third, it might show that if the right were so defined, then the cost to society would not simply be incremental, but would be of a degree far beyond the cost paid to grant the original right, a degree great enough to justify whatever assault on dignity or equality might be involved.[99]

The first point suggests that, although in principle basic rights should trump the public interest, this priority may not be axiomatic as one moves out from core cases to peripheral cases in which the right appears to be engaged. The second point, on conflicting individual rights, is discussed further in section (iv) below. It is the third point that is of greatest interest here—the concession, by a theorist who rejects the simple balancing of rights against the public interest, that there might be (extreme) circumstances in which a fundamental right could be over-trumped by public interest considerations. Dworkin expresses these circumstances in a way that is tied closely to the reasoning which led to recognition of the individual interests protected by the right, and which is intended to erect a strong presumption against allowing curtailment of a basic right. In this way, he remains confident that one can speak of fundamental rights even when providing for (some of) them to be over-trumped *in extremis*.

This approach has strong attractions for me, but I recognise that rights theories are acutely controversial. In the context of the present lecture I can at least hold on to the handrails that form part of the architecture of the European Convention itself. I can recognise that rights may have different strengths, and argue that there should be a minimum "kit" for a basic right. Thus the Convention seems to indicate three levels of strength of its rights. The first consists of the non-derogable rights: Article 15 of the Convention declares that there are some rights which must be upheld in all circumstances, no matter how dire the political situation, no matter whether there is a state of war or a "public emergency threatening the life of the nation." The non-derogable rights are the right to life (Article 2), the right not to be subjected to torture or inhuman or degrading treatment (Article 3), the right not to be subjected to forced labour (Article 4.1), and the right not to be subjected to retrospective criminal laws or penalties (Article 7). The fact that they are non-derogable indicates that they are the most basic of the funda-mental rights in the Convention. Of course, their meaning and reach are subject to interpretation, and in that sense they are not absolute—or, at least, not until the scope of their application has been determined—but it is plain that they are not intended to give way to "public interest" considerations.

Another category of Convention rights might be termed qualified or prima facie rights—the right is declared, but it is also declared that it may be interfered with on certain grounds, to the minimum extent possible. Examples of this are the right to respect for private life (Article 8), the right to freedom of thought and religion (Article 9), the right to freedom of expression (Article 10), and the right to freedom of assembly and association (Article 11).All these qualified rights are subject to interference, if it can be established that this is "necessary in a democratic society" on one of the stated grounds.

Lying between non-derogable rights and qualified rights is an intermediate category, which is less easy to label and less easy to assess. In the European Convention the category would include the right to liberty and security of the person (Article 5) and the right to a fair trial (Article 6). One might refer to the rights in this intermediate category as "strong rights", to demonstrate that they have a strength which is not qualified to the extent that the rights in Articles 8–11 are qualified. Indeed, in the internal logic of the Convention, this may prove to be quite a significant distinction. What it suggests is that, although strong rights are less fundamental than the non-derogable rights, any arguments for curtailing a strong right must at least be more powerful than the kind of "necessary in a democratic society" argument that is needed to establish the acceptability of interference with a qualified right.

This is a different and more nuanced approach than that of Dworkin, which was developed in the context of the United States constitution. The Convention may be said to assign different strengths to different groups of rights, with the result that the non-derogable rights are even more powerful than Dworkin's concept of a basic right, whereas the qualified rights are weaker than Dworkin's unitary concept. The suggestion here is that the "minimum kit" for a basic right should be that it be strong enough to override a simple argument that public safety would be enhanced if the right were curtailed: if the right were to give way in the face of a claim at that level, it would hardly be worthy of description as a "fundamental right". This of course means, in practical terms, that a claim should not be regarded as a basic right unless one is prepared to accord it this degree of priority or special weight. Whether this description of a right is precisely that which is implicit in the European Convention itself is a matter for debate: I would argue that it is clearly compatible with the structure and interpretation of the non-derogable rights and the strong rights, but there is room for disagreement about the structure and interpretation of qualified rights such as those in Articles 8–11. Those Articles allow interference where it is "necessary in a democratic society" and, although the Court has articulated principles of proportionality and subsidiarity in its application of that crucial phrase, it is true that the list of possible grounds for interference is extensive and broadly phrased. Perhaps the most appropriate summation at this stage is that the European Convention has the structure and potential to be applied in this way, but also (in respect of the qualified rights) the potential to be interpreted in a way that dilutes their application to an extent which might be taken to undermine their status as fundamental rights.

(iv) Victims' rights and the public interest

A further problem concerns the rights of victims and potential victims. It can be argued that many of the collisions I have mentioned are not between individual rights and some general "public interest" or interest in public safety, but rather between the rights of some individuals (suspects and defendants) and the rights of other individuals (victims and potential victims). Indeed, as we saw above, Dworkin argues that, in principle, individual rights can only be curtailed by other individual rights with which they conflict, and not by broader public interest considerations except *in extremis*.[100] The Convention itself allows certain individual rights (such as the qualified rights in Articles 8–11) to be curtailed either "for the protection of the rights and freedoms of others", or by reference to public interest factors such as national security, the prevention of crime and disorder, and other stipulated heads of justification which are held to be "necessary in a democratic society". The focus here will be on the former, exploring the proposition that a right can be curtailed if it conflicts with or threatens to curtail another individual right.

Why is this argument potentially more powerful? In the first place, it is capable of giving rise to the curtailment of stronger rights such as the right to confront witnesses. Thus in *Doorson v. Netherlands*[101] the Court held that, where there were credible and specific dangers of reprisals (one of the two witnesses had been attacked before by a drug dealer against whom he had testified, and the other had been threatened on this occasion),[102] the protection of the witnesses' right to security of person under Article 5 should be allowed to detract from the defendant's right to confrontation under Article 6(3)(d), although to the minimum extent feasible. This is an important decision for many reasons. The Court recognised the clash of individual rights, and was concerned to ensure that the right of the defendant at the criminal trial was maintained as fully as possible, whilst ensuring that the rights of the witness received due protection. Thus the Court insisted on allowing procedures designed to ensure protection of the physical security of the witnesses, procedures which inevitably curtailed the defendant's right under Article 6(3)(d); but the Court also insisted that the defendant's right should be curtailed to the minimum extent possible, and that "the handicaps under which the defence laboured [must be] sufficiently counterbalanced by the procedures followed by the judicial authorities."[103] This landmark decision establishes the principle of minimum interference with the rights of a defendant, and also that of other safeguards to compensate for any necessary impairment of the initial right. The Court's approach does use the term "balance" (or at least "counterbalancing"), but it also sets out some distinct parameters for such reasoning.

This leads to the question of whether it would be possible to use this reasoning as a template for some of the "public interest" cases, arguing that it is not so much a wide public interest but rather the rights of potential victims that are in conflict with the defendant's rights. Some might argue that dealing in hard drugs is a potential threat to the right to life or physical security of those who buy the drugs, and that this might justify restrictions on defence rights in drugs cases. Arguments of that kind meet formidable obstacles, in terms of both the consent of drug users to what they are doing and the degree of risk to life and physical integrity which consumption of the drug presents. Leaving aside the consent point, significant as it is, we should recall that in *Doorson* there were credible grounds for accepting that there was an immediate risk of physical attack. This is a long way from the typical drug dealing case, in terms of violations of Convention rights of victims. How do we deal with probabilities here? Three propositions may be advanced:

(1) First, we are discussing whether a Convention right of the defendant's should be curtailed: the starting point is therefore that an actual curtailment of the defendant's right has to be justified.

(2) Secondly, the certainty that the defendant's right would be curtailed ought to require, if not equal certainty, a high probability that a Convention right of a victim would be

violated as a result of applying normal criminal procedure or by some other State action, if the defendant's right were not curtailed. It would not be acceptable to allow a sure violation of the defendant's right on the basis of a possible violation of the victim's right. On the other hand, in the unusual case where there is a probability that the Convention rights of two or more victims might be violated, it is particularly difficult to weigh that against the certain curtailment of the defendant's right(s).

(3) Thirdly, and even without the awkward issue of multiple potential victims, the key question turns on degrees of probability of rights infringements. There will always be empirical-factual questions, but the normative question is what degree of probability of violating another's rights should be required before actually curtailing a defendant's right. Surely the least degree that would be acceptable would be a finding that the prospective violation of the victim's right is more probable than not, which will be rare indeed.[104] An alternative approach, recognising the State's duty to ensure that there are laws and systems which protect the human rights of all citizens,[105] would be to argue that restrictions may only be placed on a defendant's right where Dworkin's second condition[106] is met—that a loss of utility of extraordinary dimensions would occur if the right were maintained without abridgement.

How might these propositions apply to the types of case discussed in these lectures? In serious fraud cases there is no question of imminent danger to the rights of others under Articles 2, 3 or 5: although the right to property under Protocol 1 might be threatened, this is a qualified right which surely should not weigh heavily against the right to a fair trial under Article 6. It is quite clear that almost all drug trafficking cases, except those where very young people are targeted, will fail the probability test: the harm in most such cases is more speculative and more remote. However, if it is shown that the case involves organised crime, as in *Doorson* itself, this might give rise to a perceived threat to witnesses, although we must recall that in many earlier cases (see part B of this chapter) it was held that the potential threat was insufficient to justify witness anonymity which deprived the defence of the right to confrontation conferred by Article 6(3)(d). What was unusual about *Doorson* was the evidence of previous and/or direct threats to the two witnesses: it cannot be enough to argue that, because the case allegedly involves a criminal organisation, it can be assumed that witnesses may be threatened and therefore the defence's rights should be curtailed. Only where the risk is shown to be sufficiently imminent to be regarded as more probable than not to materialise, it is submitted, is there sufficient ground to consider even the minimal curtailment of an Article 6 right that *Doorson* permitted.

It is no argument to say that the rights of the innocent should be given greater weight than the rights of criminals, because we are dealing here with rights that operate before or during the criminal trial—at a time when the presumption of innocence in Article 6(2) applies, and defendants have not been convicted. Moreover, the above analysis makes it clear that there must be an assessment of the potential threat to rights in each case: as has been held in several Convention contexts,[107] it cannot be sufficient to regard a whole category of cases as presenting danger (*e.g.* organised crime, drug trafficking), in a way that fails to recognise the need for each case to be assessed individually.

(v) The problem of conflicting "public interests"

We have just explored the extent to which one individual right may properly be curtailed so as to protect another individual right, and a procedural schema for reasoning of this kind was proposed. However, in many cases it is not possible to regard the conflict as one between the rights of individuals, and so the question of clashes between public interests and fundamental rights must be addressed. It was argued above that the recognition of fundamental rights is not necessarily inconsistent with respect for the value of democratic processes. There was then exploration of the extent to which one can meaningfully speak of human rights or fundamental rights and still allow considerations of the public interest to override them in certain circumstances. It was argued that, in principle these circumstances ought to be extreme, and the criteria should be carefully circumscribed so that the essence of the right is preserved. This should certainly be the position in respect of Articles 5 and 6, which are the focus here. The qualified rights under the Convention allow "public interest" considerations to prevail in a wider range of cases than this, and there the issue is how faithfully the courts interpret the grounds for curtailment.

E. HUMAN RIGHTS AND THE CRITICS

In this connection, it is worth asking whether some of the sharpest criticisms of human rights documents—and particularly of documents such as the European Convention—apply equally to the procedural rights which form the focus of these lectures. Those criticisms are often aimed at the individualistic nature of the rights (arguing that they neglect both the responsibilities of citizenship and wider social and economic rights), at the absolutism with which they are put forward, and at the consequent heightening of expectations of what rights can promise.[108] If one applies these criticisms to rights such as the right of a detained person to be brought promptly before a court, the presumption of innocence, the right of access to a lawyer and so forth, their force is somewhat blunted. These rights to fair criminal procedures *are* essentially individualistic, since they are intended to safeguard the position of an individual who finds herself or himself in the hands of State officials and confronted with a criminal charge. There is nothing in these individual rights that is inherently incompatible with the recognition of wider social and political rights: indeed, in several human rights documents, such as the Charter of Fundamental Rights of the European Union (2000), the different kinds of right sit side by side in a single, integrated declaration.

To assert that these procedural rights are essentially individualistic is not to ignore the possibility of conflicts between these rights and other significant interests. Rather than accusing human rights advocates of "absolutism", a more telling criticism might be that qualifications or exceptions to rights tend to be accepted too readily. For example, the privilege against self-incrimination is declared without qualification in Article 14 of the International Covenant on Civil and Political Rights,[109] and yet there is much debate over the extent to which it might justifiably be restricted in certain spheres (such as a car owner's duty to declare who was driving the car at a particular time) where many countries feel that it is in the general interest to impose this responsibility on those who are car owners, as a means of enhancing road safety and ensuring the detection of offenders. Insofar as these arguments for restricting procedural rights are successful, it may well follow that the rhetoric of rights leads people to expect far greater protection than in fact it delivers. Thus, the strongest criticism to strike at the criminal procedure rights in Article 5 and 6 is that they may promise far more than they deliver in practice.

There may be an even sharper criticism here. It may not simply be that realities fail to match the rhetoric. It can be argued that the rhetoric and the logic of human rights are flawed, because they are not even self-consistent. It is a fundamental proposition that a legal system must not contain any contradictions. Put in its most stark form, it must not command a citizen not to do X and also command her or him to do X. Transferred to the present context, this means that a legal system must not both proclaim certain rights as human rights and yet condone other laws or decisions which countenance breaches of those rights. Indeed, pressed further, a principle of coherence ought to lead to a legal system that contains mutually supporting rules and principles.[110] Thus, a system which proclaims its adherence to the human rights standards in the European Convention must not contain any rules, whether introduced by statute or by judicial decision, which are not consistent with the protection of one of the human rights declared. This is an aspect of the integrity principle—that states cannot claim to respect human rights if they have laws that are incompatible with those rights, and that courts cannot claim moral standing if they are prepared to base judgments and verdicts on evidence obtained through violations of human rights.

Even if this is acceptable as general doctrine, its application depends on resolving the inevitable indeterminacies. Thus, as we saw in part D9 of the first lecture, there is a stark question of what amounts to an inconsistency, and the problems this brings can be explored with the assistance of two examples. First, would it be inconsistent to declare that an individual has a right not to be subjected to torture and inhuman or degrading treatment (Article 3), and yet to hold that someone convicted mainly on evidence stemming from such treatment has had a fair trial (Article 6)? The question can be answered in at least two ways. In the narrowest sense, it might be said, there is no inconsistency because the violation of the Article 3 right can be compensated for, by way of monetary damages, and then the fairness of the trial is an entirely separate matter. The suspect is mistreated and suffers a violation of Article 3 rights, the resulting evidence is relied upon at trial to return a conviction, and then the suspect/offender is awarded damages for the breach of the Article 3 right. This is claimed to show adequate respect for Article 3: the fairness of the trial itself is a separate matter. An alternative view is that a court which acts on the product of a violation of the Convention perpetrates a contradiction of values. It is impossible both to subscribe to fundamental rights and not to do so. Moreover, in instrumental terms, the pronouncements of the courts carry an inevitable symbolism, and it would damage the moral standing of the courts if they were to base their decisions on evidence resulting from violations of fundamental rights, since it would undermine the authority of those rights. Indeed, since the investigators who violated Article 3 are officials of the same system which then brings the prosecution against the suspect, the prosecution would surely be tainted by the earlier breach and should not be allowed to proceed.

The latter approach was adopted by the European Commission of Human Rights where there was a breach of Article 3.[111] The Commission's view was that Article 6 would be violated if a court "subsequently accepted as evidence any admissions extorted in this manner", *i.e.* by maltreatment involving a violation of Article 3.[112] The Court has not had an opportunity to confirm this approach, but it has dealt with cases where evidence has been obtained by a breach of Article 8.[113] Here it has taken the former approach, holding that the admissibility of improperly obtained evidence is a matter for national law and that it does not necessarily render the trial unfair.[114] It remains unclear whether this is a genuinely new approach, departing from the Commission's earlier application of Article 3 in the context of Article 6, or whether the Court would distinguish between breaches of Article 3, which is a non-derogable right, and breaches of Article 8, which is merely a qualified Convention right, in their impact on the fairness of a trial. It seems that some European countries apply the stronger principle to breaches of Article 5 (evidence obtained under threat of unlawful detention) as well as breaches of Article 3.[115] The arguments for and against have already been discussed above[116]; to some extent they have empirical foundations (how would one establish that the courts' integrity would be damaged?), but their basic thrust is doctrinal. Even those who do not subscribe to the notion of fundamental human rights are likely to agree that all forms of constitutional democracy must accept a range of process values together with some vague notions of freedom and equality. Among those process values might be respect for human dignity (no torture, etc.), procedural fairness (equality of arms, etc.), rule-of-law principles (published rules to guide officials and citizens, etc.), and procedural rationality (consideration of evidence, and reasoned decisions). To the extent that some such process values are recognised, questions of consistency and moral standing re-emerge.

A second question arising from the definition of inconsistency concerns Articles 8–11 of the Convention, and other "qualified" rights in the Protocols. These are the least powerful rights in the Convention, in that paragraph 1 declares the right and then paragraph 2 sets out certain conditions under which it may be justifiably interfered with. Thus paragraph 2 of Article 8 refers to interferences "in the interests of national security, public safety or the economic well-being of the country, for the prevention of disorder or crime, for the protection of health or morals, or for the protection of the rights or freedoms of others." These are very wide sources of justification, and it might be thought that the overall qualification that any interference must be "necessary in a democratic society" might be similarly elastic. However, the limiting clauses have been interpreted by the Strasbourg Court in a way that makes the justifications more concrete and more circumscribed, by adding further conditions in cases where an interference is held to be justified—notably, the principle that any interference must be proportionate to the justification, and no more extensive. At one level, this may appear to be a legal sleight of hand: the right is declared, but public interest arguments are allowed to detract from it to the extent of allowing interference. It is a fundamental right, and a not-right, at the same time. A more constructive way of viewing the process is to suggest that it embodies a recognition of the inevitability of these clashes between individual rights and public interest; that the structure of the Convention provides for distinct methods of resolving those conflicts, by means of concepts that have some flexibility and also a solid core; and that it therefore succeeds in preserving the significance of the individual right whilst allowing incursions on it in certain kinds of situation. On this view, which is somewhat weaker than the Dworkinian approach outlined earlier but which still shares some characteristics of that approach,[117] to allow a right to be overridden or interfered with does not extinguish or weaken that right, so long as the right prevails in all cases except those in which the fairly demanding tests for interference are met.

Both of these examples, however, show the contestable nature of inconsistency in this context. They both turn, ultimately, on interpretations by judges. These interpretations should ideally be faithful to the structure of the Convention. That structure, discussed above, indicates that the process of interpreting the strong rights in Articles 5 and 6 in the light of public interest considerations should be much more stringent and restrictive than that of deciding whether an interference with a qualified right can be justified (under Article 8–11, for example). However, this is not an approach that has been taken by most

British courts so far,[118] as we saw in part C above. It is the prevailing approach in Strasbourg, as was evident in parts A and B above, but the Strasbourg Court has sometimes, and without particular justification, adopted a more flexible stance.

A prime example of this "flexibility" is the presumption of innocence: the jurisprudence of the European Court and Commission of Human Rights on Article 6(2) is rather sketchy, but it also contains several decisions allowing reverse onus provisions for reasons that are capable of applying over a wide range of offences and therefore of substantially undermining the presumption itself.[119] Similarly in Canada the Supreme Court has upheld reverse onus provisions, on public interest grounds, in relation to the possession of gun licences because of the importance of gun control,[120] in relation to being drunk in charge of a vehicle because of "the threat to public safety posed by drinking and driving"[121]; and in relation to living on the earnings of prostitution because of the need to protect prostitutes, who are "a particularly vulnerable segment of society."[122] These and other decisions may or may not appear justifiable in their specific context. But, taken together, they undermine the presumption of innocence by expanding the public interest exception in such a way that it could swallow up the principle itself. Many criminal offences are created in order to enhance public safety, or to protect vulnerable sectors of society. Very few offences of violence or sexual offences would fail to fulfil these criteria, and yet the whole purpose of the presumption of innocence is to protect people accused of crimes, for the reasons outlined in the first lecture. Justifications for making exceptions cannot be reasons which apply generally, since general reasons would be inconsistent with the principle itself.

Does this acknowledgement that there are controversial elements in human rights, in terms of the extent to which they ought to give way to public interest arguments, destroy the claim that fundamental rights have some kind of objective validity, over and above the changing output of legislatures? This question makes little sense unless one has a good idea of what is meant by "objective validity". Probably in this context it is another way of describing the foundational quality of claims and interests that come to be recognised as "rights": can one describe a right as fundamental and then accept that it is not so fundamental that it cannot give way to public interest considerations in certain contexts? The problem may be that certain human rights are sometimes described as absolute when in practice they are not—a problem of exaggeration, a problem of language—but there is also a deeper issue about the development and interpretation of rights. It would be wrong to assume that rights ought to be unchanging. The European Convention on Human Rights is distinctly a product of the historical moment when it was drafted. The primary concerns in the aftermath of the Second World War were deeply felt, but were focused on then recent events.[123] The Convention may be thought to be deficient insofar as it purports to identify, within the narrow context of criminal procedure, those rights which ought to be recognised as sufficiently fundamental to be declared in this supra-national document. To take a few simple examples, the Convention does not deal with rights relating to the taking of DNA and other samples, to the use of deceptive practices by the police, and to the rights of victims—three issues which have come to the fore in recent years.

There is, of course, a means for dealing with this "time-warp" argument, and that is the doctrine of the European Court of Human Rights that the Convention should be treated as a "living instrument", and developed in response to changing circumstances. There are plenty of examples of the Court developing the text of the Convention so as to deal with new or neglected issues,[124] and also to respond to changing social attitudes and perceptions.[125] Yet the possibilities that this doctrine opens up are taken by some to undermine the whole human rights endeavour. The democratic principle is undermined, because it transpires that the human rights document (be it a constitution, bill of rights or the Convention) is not a set of constraints imposed by the legislature on itself but rather an open-ended text which can be developed by others in directions which were unforeseen by those who introduced the document. This is particularly true where the courts develop implied extensions or exceptions to the declared rights. As Costas Douzinas has argued:

> The legal principles of human rights adjudication are beset by squatting parasitical counter-principles (for example, free speech against national security or the protection of privacy) . . . and the absence of any meta-principle to guide rational choice.[126]

There are, as we have seen, plenty of "public interest" arguments "squatting" beside the Convention rights relating to criminal procedure, and being allowed by some courts in some circumstances to eat into those declared rights. There is no "meta-principle" to guide the courts in deciding whether or not to accede to arguments in favour of restricting a right, but that is probably too much to expect. An honest human rights advocate could surely not deny that there is an element of indeterminacy in human rights declarations. Indeed, some regard this as a merit: Lord Williams of Mostyn argued "that a general description of rights is in many ways much more appropriate than an attempted description or prescription of rights which is not capable of being flexible with changing social conditions."[127]

This is a position that raises important questions which have been signalled but not discussed fully in this lecture. One of those questions concerns the body that should take these decisions. Was Lord Williams of Mostyn assuming that the judiciary would be the arbiters of the flexibility of Convention rights, or was he assuming that both Parliament and the judiciary would be able to take advantage of this flexibility? The "creative tension" that the Human Rights Act sets up between legislature and judiciary[128] raises serious questions about the role of the (unelected) judiciary in this process.[129] Almost inevitably it will be the judges of the higher courts who adjudicate on the limits to which Convention rights can be pushed, even if it is the legislature that originally does the pushing. It will usually, therefore, fall to the judiciary to determine the directions of the "flexibility" to which Lord Williams referred. No doubt the best way of responding to Douzinas is to argue that there must be open and principled argument about developments of, or restrictions on, human rights. It is possible to develop criteria, and reasoning procedures, which place limiting structures on judicial interpretation without inhibiting all flexibility. This does not dispose of the Douzinas critique, but rather accepts the inevitability of the absence of a guiding meta-principle and suggests that, with other checks and balances in place, it may be possible to ensure that human rights declarations are interpreted in some form of principled manner. This is not to represent the content of fundamental rights as being in a constant state of flux, but to recognise that there are likely to be frequent adjustments and pressures to re-appraise the scope of particular rights. These are not essentially legal decisions to be taken by the courts: many of them are as political as the original decision to introduce the Human Rights Act, bearing out the argument of Martin Loughlin that one of the Act's effects will be to increase the "legalization" of political debate and the "politicization" of legal decision-making.[130] In the third lecture we look more closely at some of the arguments typically used by politicians and judges who purport to be engaged in what they regard as the necessary "balancing" process.

[1] (1978) 2 E.H.R.R. 214; the "national security" justification for interference with Article 8 rights was also considered by the European Commission on Human Rights in the later case of *Esbester v. U.K.* (1993) 18 E.H.R.R. CD 72.

[2] *ibid.*, para. 48.

[3] *ibid.*, para. 49.

[4] *ibid.*, para. 56.

[5] (1988) 11 E.H.R.R. 117.

[6] *ibid.*, para. 62.

[7] (1990) 13 E.H.R.R. 157.

[8] *ibid.*, para. 32.

[9] *ibid.*, para. 35.

[10] (1994) 19 E.H.R.R. 193.

[11] *ibid.*, para. 47.

[12] *Fox* (1992) 14 E.H.R.R. 108, at para. 28, citing *Brogan* (1989) 11 E.H.R.R. 117, para. 48.

[13] *R v. D.P.P. ex p. Kebilene* [1999] 3 W.L.R. 972, at p. 994D.

[14] See *Brannigan and McBride v. U.K.* (1993) 17 E.H.R.R. 539, paras 59–65.

[15] Such as *Margaret Murray* (above, n.10), and *O'Hara v. U.K.*, judgment of October 16, 2001.

[16] Another example of this is to be found in *Aksoy v. Turkey* (1997) 23 E.H.R.R. 553, where the Court reiterated that "the investigation of terrorist offences undoubtedly presents the authorities with special problems", but it found clear violations of the Article 5(3) right to be brought promptly before a court and held that the exigencies of the situation which had led Turkey to derogate from that Article did not justify such lengthy detention (14 days) without access to a court or a lawyer.

[17] (1989) 12 E.H.R.R. 434.

[18] *ibid.*, para. 41, citing *Barbera, Messegue and Jabardo v. Spain* (1989) 11 E.H.R.R. 360, para. 78.

[19] *ibid.*, para. 44.

[20] (1990) 13 E.H.R.R. 281.

[21] (1993) 17 E.H.R.R. 251.

[22] *ibid.*, para. 44.

[23] (1996) 22 E.H.R.R. 330.

[24] *ibid.*, para. 72; a similar judgment was delivered in *Van Mechelen v. Netherlands* (1997) 25 E.H.R.R. 647 (see paras 52–54), but in that case the Court held that Article 6 had been violated.

[25] See the discussion in Chap. 1, section D8.

[26] *Saunders v. U.K.* (1996) 23 E.H.R.R. 313, para. 68; to the same effect, see the earlier decision in *Murray v. U.K.* (1996) 22 E.H.R.R. 29, para. 45, and *Condron v. U.K.* (2001) 31 E.H.R.R. 1, para. 47.

[27] *Saunders v. U.K.* (1996) 23 E.H.R.R. 313, p. 329.

[28] *ibid.*, pp. 329–330. The Commission voted by 14 to 1 that Article 6 had been violated.

[29] (1996) 23 E.H.R.R. 313, para. 74.

[30] Notably in *John Murray v. U.K.* (1996) 22 E.H.R.R. 29, at para. 47; see the discussion in Chap. 1, part D3.

[31] (2000) 33 E.H.R.R. 264.

[32] *ibid.*, para. 58.

[33] (1999) 28 E.H.R.R. 101.

[34] *ibid.*, para. 36.

[35] It is also noticeable that when in its subsequent judgment in *Khan v. U.K.* (2001) 31 E.H.R.R. 45 the Court referred to its decision in *Teixeira*, it referred to

it (para. 34, n.5) as a case "in a different context", and failed to mention that a violation of Article 6 was found in that case.
36 *e.g.* Lord Bingham in *Brown v. Stott* [2001] 2 W.L.R. 817, p. 825.
37 *e.g.* in *Soering v. U.K.* (1989) 11 E.H.R.R. 439 the Court said that "inherent in the whole Convention is a search for a fair balance between the demands of the general interest of the community and the requirements of the protection of the individual's fundamental rights" (para. 89); and, to the same effect, *Sporrong and Lonnroth v. Sweden* (1982) 5 E.H.R.R. 35, para. 69. These dicta have been much cited by British judges.
38 (1988) 13 E.H.R.R. 379.
39 See the discussion of *Lambert* and other decisions in lecture 1, above, p. 17.
40 *Brown v. Stott* [2001] 2 W.L.R. 817, at pp. 825–827.
41 (1989) 12 E.H.R.R. 434.
42 See also, *e.g. Windisch v. Austria* (1990) 13 E.H.R.R. 281, *Saidi v. France* (1993) 17 E.H.R.R. 251.
43 *Doorson v. Netherlands* (1996) 22 E.H.R.R. 330, esp. para. 74; *cf. van Mechelen v. Netherlands* (1997) 25 E.H.R.R. 647, where the procedures were insufficient and breach of Article 6(3)(d) was found.
44 *e.g.* Lord Bingham in *Brown v. Stott* [2001] 2 W.L.R. 817, at p. 826, and Lord Clyde at p. 840; Lord Hope in *A.* [2001] 2 W.L.R. 1546, at para. 91.
45 (1985) 7 E.H.R.R. 528, para. 57.
46 *Rowe and Davis v. U.K.* (2000) 30 E.H.R.R. 1, at para. 61.
47 Above, n. 43 and accompanying text.
48 A recent affirmation of this may be found in *Brennan v. U.K.* [2002] Crim.L.R. 214, on the right of access to a lawyer. For general discussion, see Emmerson and Ashworth, paras 2–60 to 2–67; see also K. Starmer, *European Human Rights Law* (LAG, 1999), pp. 182–185; P. van Dijk and G. van Hoof, *Theory and Practice of the European Convention on Human Rights* (3rd ed., Kluwer, 1999), pp. 427–428.
49 The House of Lords has noted that the proportionality requirement under Article 8 is significantly more demanding than the *Wednesbury* test: *R. (on the application of Daly) v. Home Secretary* [2001] 2 W.L.R. 1622, *per* Lord Steyn at para. 27.
50 It seems likely that this doctrine has its origins in the German constitutional notion of the *Wesengehaltgarantie*, which is supposed to guarantee an inviolable core of each right, setting a limit beyond which it may not be restricted. However, some commentators argue that in practice this affords no significant protection, beyond the overriding principle of respect for human dignity in the German *Grundgesetz*. I am grateful to Liora Lazarus for this information.
51 For examples, see the discussion of the *Brogan* and *Fox, Campbell and Hartley* decisions in part A of this lecture. See also D. Friedman, "Defending the Essence of the Right: Judicial Discretion and the Human Rights Act 1998" [2001] 4 *Archbold News* 6.
52 *e.g.* in *Winterwerp v. Netherlands* (1979) 2 E.H.R.R. 387, at para. 60; *cf.* R. Clayton and H. Tomlinson, *The Law of Human Rights* (Oxford U.P., 2000), paras 6.118—6.122, who illustrate the application of "the doctrine of inherent limitations" by reference to decisions mostly on the right of access to courts.
53 The first explicit statement on this is found in *John Murray v. U.K.* (1996) 22 E.H.R.R. 29, at para. 45, citing Article 14 of the International Covenant on Civil and Political Rights.
54 [2001] 2 W.L.R. 817.
55 (1996) 22 E.H.R.R. 29, para. 47.
56 (1997) 23 E.H.R.R. 313, paras 69 and 74.
57 [2001] 2 W.L.R. 817, p. 837.
58 Above, n. 43.

[59] Above, n. 38 and accompanying text.
[60] (2000) 33 E.H.R.R. 264; see also *Quinn v. Ireland*, judgment of December 21, 2000.
[61] *ibid.*, para. 52.
[62] (1993) 16 E.H.R.R. 297.
[63] [2001] Crim.L.R. 748.
[64] For a particularly strong display of "balancing" language, see the speech of Lord Hope in *A.* [2001] 2 W.L.R. 1546; more generally, see the discussion in Arlidge, Eady and Smith, *Contempt* (2nd ed., Sweet & Maxwell, 1999), paras 2–146 to 2–150.
[65] The Court referred, in support, to its previous decisions to the same effect in *Brogan v. U.K.* (1988) 11 E.H.R.R. 117 (terrorism) and *Saunders v. U.K.* (1996) 23 E.H.R.R. 313, para. 74 (serious fraud).
[66] One of the primary justifications advanced by Lord Bingham in *Brown v. Stott* [2001] 2 W.L.R. 817, p. 836.
[67] In fact, the available sentences include a fine, penalty points and discretionary disqualification from driving.
[68] I am grateful to Colm Campbell for suggesting this reading of the decisions.
[69] Above, n. 43.
[70] In that case the Court held that exceptions to Article 6(2) should be kept within reasonable limits, "which take account of the importance of what is at stake": (1988) 13 E.H.R.R. 379, para. 28. What was at stake was a possible sentence of imprisonment, but that was not thought sufficiently important in *Salabiaku*, whereas it is clearly of great importance in the self-incrimination decisions.
[71] This appears from the approval of *Funke* in *Heaney and McGuinness v. Ireland* (2000) 33 E.H.R.R. 264, para. 49.
[72] As Lord Bingham noted in *Brown v. Stott* [2001] 2 W.L.R., p. 837. For an analysis of reasons for drawing the distinction, *cf.* S. Easton, *The Case for the Right to Silence* (2nd ed., Ashgate, 1998), Chap. 8, and D.J. Seidman and A. Stein, "The Right to Silence helps the Innocent", (2000) 114 Harv.L.R. 431.
[73] Among the recent Strasbourg authorities, see *Howarth v. U.K.* (2001) 31 E.H.R.R. 37 and, on the point from which time begins to run, *Heaney and McGuinness v. Ireland* (2000) 33 E.H.R.R. 264.
[74] [2000] 2 Cr.App.R. 445, *per* Lord Steyn.
[75] [2000] 1 W.L.R. 2396, *per* Lord Hutton.
[76] [2001] EWCA Crim. 1568.
[77] See n. 73 above.
[78] [2001] EWCA Crim. 1568, para. 19.
[79] On which, see B. Emmerson and A. Ashworth, *Human Rights and Criminal Justice* (Sweet & Maxwell, 2001), paras 14–53 to 14–56.
[80] [2001] 2 W.L.R. 779.
[81] *ibid.*, p. 809.
[82] (1988) 13 E.H.R.R. 379.
[83] [2001] 3 W.L.R. 206.
[84] On which see R. Clayton, "Regaining a Sense of Proportion: the Human Rights Act and the Proportionality Principle" [2001] E.H.R.L.R. 504.
[85] Above, n. 5; see also *Aksoy v. Turkey* (above, n.16).
[86] Above, n. 60.
[87] Notably the right to legal assistance, the limited qualification on which was recently re-affirmed in *Brennan v. U.K.* [2002] Crim.L.R. 214, and the right to disclosure of the prosecution case file, set out in *Rowe and Davis v. U.K.* (2000) 30 E.H.R.R. 1 and discussed below, p. 129.
[88] See the stimulating discussion, related to the subject of this lecture, by A. McHarg, "Reconciling Human Rights and the Public Interest" (1999) 62 M.L.R. 671.

[89] In the present context, the adjectives "fundamental", "basic" and "human" will be used interchangeably; and all references to rights should be construed as references to these fundamental rights, rather than to rights merely arising under ordinary rules of law.

[90] A similar reply can be made to the argument that to give these powers over legislation to unelected judges is anti-democratic: insofar as the power is given to the judiciary by legislation, it is democratically conferred and can, equally, be democratically altered or taken away.

[91] M. Loughlin, "Rights, Democracy and Law", in T. Campbell, K.D. Ewing and A. Tomkins (eds), *Sceptical Essays on Human Rights* (Oxford U.P., 2001), p. 42.

[92] See the discussion by T. Campbell, "Human Rights: a Culture of Controversy", (1999) 26 J.L.S. 6, esp. p. 25.

[93] H.L. Deb., vol. 582, col. 1228.

[94] For discussion of positive obligations, see Emmerson and Ashworth, *Human Rights and Criminal Justice*, Chap. 18.

[95] I am grateful to Liora Lazarus for this point. Elaboration may be found in K. Sontheimer, "Principles of Human Dignity in the Federal Republic", in K. Stern (ed.), *Germany and its Basic Law* (1993) p. 213.

[96] H.L. Deb., vol. 582, col. 1234.

[97] M. Hunt, "The Human Rights Act and Legal Culture: the Judiciary and the Legal Profession" (1999) 26 J.L.S. 86, p. 88.

[98] See Ashworth, "Criminal Proceedings after the Human Rights Act: the First Year", [2001] Crim.L.R. 855 at pp. 862–863.

[99] R.M. Dworkin, *Taking Rights Seriously* (Duckworth, 1977), p. 200.

[100] *ibid.*

[101] (1996) 22 E.H.R.R. 330, quoted above, at n. 23.

[102] *ibid.*, para. 71.

[103] *ibid.*, para. 72.

[104] Others would impose a higher threshold: thus A.E. Bottoms and R. Brownsword, "The Dangerousness Debate after the Floud Report" (1982) 22 B.J.Crim. 229 argue that there must be proof of a "vivid danger" to the potential victim's rights before any curtailment of the offender's right should be contemplated. The analysis in the text above adopts part of their reasoning (see pp. 240–241), but also recognises the force of the counter-argument of Andrew von Hirsch, *Censure and Sanctions* (Oxford U.P., 1993), p. 51.

[105] For elaboration of the positive duties of states, see Emmerson and Ashworth, *Human Rights and Criminal Justice*, Chap. 18.

[106] See above, pp. 74–75.

[107] See, *e.g. C.C. v. U.K.* [1999] Crim.L.R. 228 on refusing bail, and the English decision in *Offen (No. 2)* [2001] 1 Cr.App.R. 372 on life imprisonment for serious repeat offenders.

[108] For examples, see M.A. Glendon, *Rights Talk: the Impoverishment of Political Discourse* (Free Press, 1991), a critique of tendencies in the U.S., and A. Hutchinson, *Waiting for Coraf: a Critique of Law and Rights* (Carswell, 1994), a more general critique based on the Canadian experience; for a development of Hutchinson's position, see his *It's All in the Game: a Nonfoundationalist Account of Law and Adjudication* (Duke U.P., 2000).

[109] As we have seen at pp. 58–61 above, it is not declared explicitly in the ECHR but has been implied into it as an integral part of the right to a fair trial established by Article 6.

[110] J. Raz, *Ethics in the Public Domain* (1994), Chap. 13.

[111] *Austria v. Italy* (1961) 4 Y.B. 116.

[112] *ibid.*, at p. 784.

[113] *Schenk v. Switzerland* (1988) 13 E.H.R.R. 242, para. 46, followed in *Khan v. U.K.* (2000) 31 E.H.R.R. 1016.

[114] The authorities are not all in the same direction, however. The decision in *Teixeira de Castro v. Portugal* (1999) 28 E.H.R.R. 101, on evidence obtained by entrapment, overrode the national law and found that the trial was unfair. See also the dissent by Judge Tulkens in *P.G. and J.H. v. U.K.*, judgment of September 25, 2001.

[115] J. Pradel, "The Criminal Justice Systems facing the Challenge of Organised Crime" (1998) 69 *Revue Internationale de Droit Pénal* 673, at p. 683 referring to the Czech Penal Code.

[116] Chap. 1, part D9.

[117] Above, pp. 74–77.

[118] See discussion of the British cases in part C of this lecture.

[119] See generally Emmerson and Ashworth, *Human Rights and Criminal Justice* (2001), Chap. 9; among the few leading decisions are *Salabiaku v. France* (1988) 13 E.H.R.R. 379 and *Phillips v. U.K.* [2001] Crim.L.R. 817.

[120] *Schwartz* [1988] 2 S.C. 443.

[121] *Whyte* [1988] 2 S.C. 3.

[122] *Downey* [1992] 2 S.C. 10. For comments on these decisions, see K. Roach, *Due Process and Victims' Rights* (Toronto U.P., 1999), pp. 104–105, and in greater detail, D.R. Stuart, *Charter Justice in Canadian Criminal Law* (2nd ed., Carswell, 1996), pp. 325–349.

[123] See the fascinating study by A.W.B. Simpson, *Human Rights and the End of Empire* (Oxford U.P., 2001).

[124] In the context of Article 6, the Court has developed an array of "implied rights" on access to justice, equality of arms, silence and self-incrimination, and so forth.

[125] For example, *Tyrer v. U.K.* (1979) 2 E.H.R.R. 1 on corporal punishment, *Dudgeon v. U.K.* (1982) 4 E.H.R.R. 149 on the criminalisation of homosexual acts between consenting adults in private, and *Doorson v. Netherlands* (1996) 22 E.H.R.R. 330 on the rights of witnesses and victims in court.

[126] C. Douzinas, "Justice and Human Rights in Postmodernity", in C. Gearty and A. Tomkins (eds), *Understanding Human Rights* (Pinter, 1996), pp. 129–130.

[127] From the debates on the second reading: H.L. Deb., vol. 582, col. 1309.

[128] The term coined by Murray Hunt: see above, n. 97 and accompanying text.

[129] *e.g.* K. Ewing, "The Human Rights Act and Parliamentary Democracy" (1999) 62 M.L.R. 79.

[130] Loughlin, above, n. 91 at pp. 56–58.

3. Taking a "Balanced" View of the Public Interest

In the second lecture I contended that the use of "public interest" arguments to outweigh the human rights protections in Article 5 and 6 of the European Convention on Human Rights is of doubtful legitimacy. I referred to several attempts by governments to circumvent or minimise the right to a fair trial, notably in arguments addressed to the European Court of Human Rights, and showed that in most cases that Court declined to give way. However, such arguments have met with greater success in the British courts since the implementation of the Human Rights Act, and I criticised the judgments in some cases for their failure to take proper account of the Strasbourg decisions and of the structure and spirit of the Convention. I also went on to show that "public interest" arguments may be less strong than some of their protagonists believe them to be.

The debates about the conflicts between individual human rights and wider public interests are not solely about judicial approaches to the Convention. On the contrary, government ministers and other politicians refer to those conflicts when explaining policy initiatives, particularly in relation to serious crime. Ministers are unlikely to admit openly to a desire to dispense with the protection of human rights.[1] It is much more likely that they would wish to proclaim that the Government respects and promotes human rights, and would then seek methods of circumventing or minimising human rights protections where possible. In this lecture I draw together five ways of avoiding human rights—developing exceptions to human rights based on the seriousness of the crime; manipulating the civil-criminal boundary; expanding the definitions of exceptional categories; propounding a "no rights without responsibilities" thesis; and arguing that the curtailment of a human right is necessary for the protection of the human rights of other individuals. The lecture begins by looking at how other countries deal with some of the types of serious crime we are discussing in these lectures, such as drug trafficking and serious fraud. The lecture will conclude with some general reflections on how to deal with the inevitable tension between the requirements of Articles 5 and 6 of the Convention and the kinds of "public interest" argument often associated with policies against serious crime.

A. AVOIDING HUMAN RIGHTS

Let me begin by introducing the five techniques of avoidance, giving slightly greater discussion to those which will not be taken up in detail later in the lecture.

(i) Developing exceptions based on serious crime:

We have already noted some evidence of this during the second lecture, particularly when discussing the general refusal of the Strasbourg Court to allow exceptions on this basis. In part C below we examine the justifications for arguing that the investigation and prosecution of serious crime should be grounds for special exceptions; there is also brief discussion of the view that human rights protections should not apply (fully) to those accused of minor or regulatory crimes.

(ii) Manipulating the civil-criminal boundary

Since most of the Article 6 safeguards, including all those set out in paragraphs 2 and 3 of Article 6, apply only to persons charged with a criminal offence, the labelling of a process as civil can have a dramatic effect in altering the position of the defendant. However, the categorisation of proceedings in domestic law has not been taken at face value in European human rights law. The Strasbourg Court has developed an autonomous meaning for terms such as "criminal charge" and "penalty", and there is now a mass of decisions demonstrating the Court's willingness to override domestic law and to rule that proceedings are criminal in substance, even if they are classified as civil in form, and that therefore the full range of Article 6 safeguards should be available to the defendant.[2]

Nevertheless, two pieces of English policy-making deliberately aimed at avoiding the human rights protections available in criminal cases have been upheld. The confiscation legislation, which enables courts to make a confiscation order in respect of property acquired in the six years before conviction of a drug trafficking offence unless the offender proves that it does not represent the proceeds of crime,[3] has been held by a majority of the European Court of Human Rights not to involve a "criminal charge."[4] The proceedings in which an anti-social behaviour order is made, under section 1 of the Crime and Disorder Act 1998, have also been held to be civil (as the legislation states) and not criminal, despite the severe penalty to which breach of the order may, and in the oft-repeated view of former Home Secretary Jack Straw *should*, result. The anti-social behaviour order was introduced, it will be recalled, specifically with the intention of circumventing the "shortcomings" of criminal proceedings, *i.e.*, the normal protection of defendants' rights before they are subjected to potentially severe sanctions.[5] More will be said about the civil/criminal boundary in part C below.

(iii) Expanding the definitions of exceptional categories

Another potential means of avoidance is to expand the definition of key concepts likely to evoke a sympathetic response from the public and from Strasbourg. We have noted that the Strasbourg Court has shown tangible recognition of the importance of taking strong measures against terrorism, even though on several occasions it has stopped short of allowing anti-terrorist measures to detract from basic rights assured by the Convention.[6] The extra strength of an argument based on terrorism makes it tempting to expand the definition of what counts as terrorism, and this is exactly what the British Government did in promoting the Terrorism Act 2000. Thus section 1 of the Act introduces a much wider concept of terrorism than existed previously, and one that might well embrace forms of so-called organised crime. Further discussion of the technique of normalising the exceptional[7] will be found in part B (iv) of this chapter.

(iv) Propounding a "no rights without responsibilities" approach

Another technique is to argue that the development of a human rights culture is only possible if citizens accept that they have certain responsibilities as well as rights. The substance and implications of this approach are examined in part D below. Suffice it to say here that, although the rhetoric of this approach chimes well with other contemporary ideas of citizenship, community and participatory democracy, it does not amount to a suggestion that people should only be accorded rights if they first show their willingness to submit to various obligations. Instead, the approach is intended chiefly to lay the ground for restrictions on, or exceptions to, individual rights in the name of the greater public good. To this extent, some of the counter-arguments already discussed in part D of the second lecture, above, become relevant.

(v) Ensuring protection for the rights of other individuals

In the text of the second paragraphs of Articles 8–11, it is recognised that the right of one individual may justifiably be curtailed if that is necessary to safeguard the rights of another. Similarly, the Strasbourg Court has recognised that certain Article 6 rights of persons accused of a criminal offence may have to be curtailed if that is necessary to protect the rights of another. Reference has already been made, in part D8 of the first lecture, to the Court's decision in *Doorson v. Netherlands*[8] to the effect that a defendant's right to confront a witness against him may be modified if the identity of that witness has to be kept secret in order to protect him or her from threats to life or physical security. It will also be recalled that the Court insisted that any such curtailment of an Article 6 right should be as minimal as possible, and should respect the rights of the defence so far as possible. The limits of this "conflict of individual rights" argument were examined in part D(iv) of the second lecture, but it remains the only one of these five means of avoiding human rights that is legitimate and within the spirit, and to some extent within the letter, of the Convention. It deals with the inevitable problem of conflicting rights although, as will be recognised more fully in the final part of this chapter, it does so without the aid of any meta-principle to resolve such conflicts in a consistent manner.

B. THE INTERNATIONAL BATTLE AGAINST SERIOUS CRIME

One of the characteristics of regional and international co-operation in matters of criminal justice is that certain themes have, in the last decade, assumed such proportions that they commonly attract the language of battle—the war on drugs, the fight against organised crime, and so forth. Indeed, there are many who argue that most of the key fields are connected—that organised crime is heavily involved in drug trafficking and in serious fraud, for example.[9] It appears that when so much energy is expended on the creation and drafting of conventions relating to criminal justice, co-operation between states on terrorism, organised crime, fraud, drugs and so forth, there is little left for the protection of human rights. The assumption seems to be that, if one accepts the need for greater and more repressive measures against these forms of criminality, on the basis that they may in some forms threaten to undermine the social fabric (one thinks here of the Mafia in Italy, and of the organisations which have reportedly sprung up in the Eastern European countries in the last decade), then one also accepts the need for tough and intrusive measures. The same discourse and the same assumptions are evident in official statements leading up to legislation on such matters in this country and in many other jurisdictions. In such a context, any "moaning" about human rights protections may be taken as evidence of an extreme and unworldly liberalism.

To its credit, the Council of Europe itself has made attempts to remain faithful to the principles of the European Convention on Human Rights in its own policy statements. Yet, even there, the strain arising from the tension between the repression of serious crime and the protection of human rights is evident. In this section, we consider some of the arguments for special treatment of certain types of offending, and some of the devices employed in different countries in order to secure special treatment.

(i) Organised Crime:

The phenomenon of organised crime has been recognised as long as the operations of the Mafia in Italy and other countries have been known. In recent years it has assumed renewed significance, in the context of drug trafficking, illegal immigration, protection rackets, and a wider range of criminal activities. In 2000 the United Nations Convention against Transnational Organised Crime was drafted. One of the objectives of the treaty is:

> to align national laws in criminalising acts committed by organised criminal groups. Under the Convention, this behaviour includes organising, directing or aiding serious offences committed by an organised criminal group. And it entails agreeing with one or more other persons to commit a serious crime for financial or other gain.[10]

The Convention (not yet in force, but open for ratification) aims to standardise not only domestic criminal offences penalising organised crime, but also offences of money laundering, corruption, and the obstruction of justice by bribery or by threats or intimidation of witnesses. It will also extend the use of "controlled delivery" from drug trafficking investigations to other forms of serious offence targeted by the Convention, and encourages the use of "special investigative techniques" such as surveillance measures and undercover operations, "if permitted by the basic principles of its domestic legal system."[11] The latter condition, it should be noted, would now encompass the Human Rights Act in this country.

In the European Union, the Treaty of Amsterdam envisages the creation of new laws to tackle "organised crime", as part of the "Third Pillar" initiatives in criminal justice. In the Council of Europe, the recommendation in favour of further and more intensive methods of detecting and investigating organised crime comes in a document which begins with the declaration that all responses to crime must be "subject to the paramount aim of guaranteeing respect for human rights."[12] It is necessary to approach such statements with scepticism, given the strong political attractions of repressive policies in these fields, and the enthusiasm of many investigators and prosecutors; but it is of some symbolic importance that the Council of Europe's official statements appear to give priority to human rights safeguards.

The legislatures of many countries have been active in this field in recent years. In Canada, Bill C–95, passed in 1997, brings together a range of powers to tackle organised crime. It includes a new offence of "participation in criminal organisation", so that where a person is reasonably suspected of committing this offence, the investigators have various powers of access to tax information, to apply to intercept communications, and to seize property. There are also enhanced maximum penalties. It remains to be seen whether these extended powers will withstand challenge under the Charter, or whether there are sufficient safeguards to satisfy the courts. One decision that has caused anxiety among investigators is *Campbell and Shirose*,[13] where the Supreme Court held a "reverse sting" police operation to be unlawful, going beyond the statutory authority for proactive policing, and stayed the prosecution. However, the Canadian government responded by proposing wider powers for law enforcement officials investigating "organized crime": Bill C–24 of 2001 seeks to achieve this, but its compatibility with the Charter will doubtless be challenged in due course.

In Germany, there are extra procedural powers relating to the interception of communications and the use of personal data which apply to certain very serious crimes, including serious

offences committed *gewerbs- oder gewohnheitsmassig* (in a commercial or habitual manner), which is the German way of
defining organised crime.[14] French law extends the period
during which a person can be subjected to custodial remand
where the charge falls into a category of seriousness that
includes terrorism, drug trafficking and *une infraction commise en
bande organisee* (an offence committed in an organised group),
which seems to be the French approach to organised crime.

One key element in contemporary policy against organised
crime in most countries is the criminalisation of money-
laundering and the provision of strong powers for the confiscation of assets. The trend in this direction, first given an author-
itative encouragement by the United Nations Convention
against Illicit Traffic in Narcotic Drugs and Psychotropic Substances (1988), is now in full spate in European countries. Some
argue that the primary purpose of organised crime is to make
profit, rather than to achieve other forms of domination,[15] a view
which supports this trend. Others, recognising the extent of the
duties now imposed on bankers and other agencies, argue that
the powers taken by many governments—in addition to other
initiatives against corruption by officials and by multinational
corporations—"aim for the control of money flows as such" and
therefore belong to a deeper agenda.[16]

On a more prosaic level, many European legislatures have
now introduced mechanisms for the confiscation of the proceeds
of crime, whether from drug trafficking or more generally. In
Ireland the Proceeds of Crime Act 1996 introduced a form of
civil forfeiture for the proceeds of crime, and the Act's constitu-
tionality has been upheld.[17] In *Welch v. United Kingdom* the
Strasbourg Court had to determine whether an order for the
confiscation of the assets of a convicted drug trafficker is a
"penalty", and held that it is because it serves punitive as well
as preventive purposes. However, the Court expressly stated
that its decision "does not call into question in any respect the
powers of confiscation conferred on the courts as a weapon in
the fight against the scourge of drug trafficking."[18] Such powers
run counter to the right to peaceful enjoyment of property
declared in Protocol 1 to the Convention, but are regarded as
falling within the "public interest" exception for which the
Protocol makes provision. Similarly, it is not unusual for confiscation laws to reverse the onus of proof, requiring the
offender to exonerate himself by showing that certain items of
property do not represent the proceeds of crime, and this has
been held compatible with the presumption of innocence in
Article 6(2) of the Convention.[19] However, the Government's

Proceeds of Crime Bill has been found by the Joint Committee on Human Rights to contain provisions which will probably be held to be incompatible with Convention rights under Articles 6, 7 and 8[20]: even if the Committee's predictions are not borne out by subsequent judicial decisions, the Bill stands as another example of the Government sailing as close to the wind as possible, rather than promoting the spirit of the Convention.

The question of organised crime is a difficult one. There is unmistakable evidence of criminal organisations at work:

> we should view organised crime as a cultural phenomenon rather than as a police problem; the local and particular manifestation of criminal collaborations, territorially rooted in multiple indicators of disadvantage, sensitive to markets yet informed by precedent.[21]

This depiction of organised crime as an outgrowth of poverty and the self-protection of the oppressed is a frequent theme, as are both the predominantly local nature of organised crime and its adaptability to the prized commodities of the day. Although organised crime clearly exists, there is an incentive for some to exaggerate its extent and significance—for law enforcement agencies to do so in order to obtain greater powers and resources, and for governments to do so in order to bolster their popularity by being seen to oppose obviously evil forces. It is also difficult to settle on a definition, and there are those who have a clear interest in expanding the definition so as to include more forms of behaviour.

A review of the press statements of the National Criminal Intelligence Service (NCIS) demonstrates the tone of many official declarations. The definition of organised crime adopted by NCIS has four elements: it applies to criminal groups:

i. which contain at least three people;

ii. whose criminal activity is prolonged or indefinite;

iii. where criminals are motivated by profit or power;

iv. where serious criminal offences are being committed.[22]

The most significant current threats from organised crime are said to fall into seven fields, which NCIS describes thus:

Class A drugs (particularly heroin, cocaine and Ecstasy)
Organised Immigration Crime
Fraud (particularly revenue fraud)
Cross-Sector Criminal Activity

Money Laundering
Paedophile Crime (including on-line child abuse)
Hi-tech crime (particularly Internet crime).

NCIS is also keen to point out that the activities of organised criminals are not confined to inner city areas. Although this does not argue against the criminological view that organised crime arises out of the poorer areas, it is intended as a warning to the middle classes:

> Let us be quite clear. Serious and organised crime is not merely 'someone else's problem,' a murky business that takes place only in the inner cities. It affects everyone in this country and its effects can be seen everywhere you go. Counterfeit currency in busy pubs; counterfeit goods sold on trestle tables in high streets; child pornography and advanced fee frauds on the Internet; and Class A drugs at teenage discos.[23]

There is not enough available evidence to judge whether assertions of this kind minimise or exaggerate the extent of the problems. What is significant in the present context is that they are presented in a way that is designed to heighten public awareness (fear), and to convey the impression that, if only the law enforcement agencies are given the powers with which to tackle organised crime, then there will be significant advances in controlling it. Indeed, the link is clear when a passage from a previous NCIS press release on the Regulation of Investigatory Powers Act is considered:

> The criminal fraternity always exploits developing technology and organised criminals are already using internet technology to increase the already substantial profits from their criminality. All we are seeking is modern tools to do a modern job.[24]

The argument in favour of extended (or "modernised")[25] powers may or may not be well founded. The key issue here is whether the human rights of persons targeted by the measures are adequately safeguarded.

Thus, nothing here suggests that some threats from organised crime ought not to be taken very seriously, and that there should not be domestic and international initiatives against it. What Jean Pradel has described as the "angelical" liberal approach of ignoring the phenomenon is not to be commended, but neither is the approach of "making an absolute priority of the fight against organised crime, without regard to principles."[26] The middle way is to devise strategies which may include the creation of new offences and new powers, whether of investigation or of confiscation, but which ensure that all the necessary safeguards under the Convention are also put in place. Greater resources should be put into the prevention of serious crime, rather than into the policing of petty crime and disorder, so as to make these policies a reality. If there are calls to grant to the police exceptional powers against those suspected of involvement in organised crime, there must be critical review of the extent of the problem and of the definition applied to "organised crime". Some years ago, the House of Commons Home Affairs Committee resolved:

> while we recognise that intelligence gathering has a vital role to play in the fight against organised crime, we do not conclude that the present situation yet calls for substantial inroads to be made into ordinary citizens' freedom from intrusion by the state.[27]

Now that the Human Rights Act is part of English law, the closing words have greater significance and the idea of making "substantial inroads" into ordinary freedom would need to be reconciled with the requirements of Article 8 and other parts of the Convention. It would be possible to tackle these forms of crime whilst preserving the integrity of the Convention by ensuring that, if a strong case is made out for extra powers, any new framework includes extra safeguards for suspects too. This point is pursued below, when considering the special measures taken in other countries.

(ii) Drug trafficking:

Following a lead from the United Nations in 1988, most countries have renewed their legislation on drugs and drug trafficking, and have taken more severe measures. In this country the maximum penalties for drug trafficking were increased by the Controlled Drugs (Penalties) Act 1985, with importation carrying life imprisonment. Since then the primary legislative effort has been in respect of confiscation of the assets of convicted drug traffickers, and various other powers of seizure and forfeiture, now contained in the Drug Trafficking Act 1994 and shortly to be consolidated in a Proceeds of Crime Act. As Lord Bingham of Cornhill put it:

> This body of legislation rests (so far as it concerns drug trafficking) on a series of important premises: that the unlawful consumption of drugs, particularly class A drugs, is a very grave, far-reaching and destructive social evil; that persistence of this evil depends on the

availability of an adequate supply of drugs for consumption; that the availability of an adequate supply of drugs in its turn depends on the activity of those who traffic in drugs by manufacturing, importing, buying and re-selling them; that those who traffic in drugs reap rich rewards from their activity; that those who traffic in drugs go to great lengths to conceal their activities, cover their tracks and conceal their assets; that the evil consequences of drug trafficking are such as properly to engage the sanctions and procedures of the criminal law; that those convicted of trafficking in drugs should be liable to imprisonment for what may be very long periods, to punish them, to prevent them offending again and to deter others from similar offending; and that it is desirable to deprive traffickers of their ill-gotten gains, so that the hope of profit is heavily outweighed by the fear of punishment. These premises are reflected in the United Nations Convention against Illicit Traffic in Narcotic Drugs and Psychotropic Substances adopted in Vienna on 19 December 1988, which the United Kingdom ratified in June 1991, and in the experience and practice of many states all over the world.[28]

Thus, as Lord Bingham suggests, the strong British laws against drug trafficking have parallels in other countries. In France, Article 222 of the *code pénal* contains a series of offences in respect of drug trafficking: the most serious offence is aimed at the organisers of drug trafficking of any kind (Article 222–34), and this is supported by a range of offences including offering drugs for sale (Article 222–39, with a maximum of five years' imprisonment, rising to ten years if the offer is made to a minor or in a place of education). The *Cour de Cassation* has upheld the validity of using *comparution immédiate* (immediate appearance in court for trial) to deal with drug smugglers found in possession by customs officers: that procedure is normally reserved for crimes with no more than a seven year maximum, and a special exception has been made for the relatively serious offence of drug trafficking.[29] In Germany special powers have been taken in order to facilitate the investigation of serious crimes such as drug trafficking. Section 98a of the *Strafprozessordnung*, introduced in 1992, allows the use of certain personal data, normally protected by the right of privacy, where there is reasonable suspicion of the person's involvement in drug trafficking. Section 100a likewise allows telephone tapping to be ordered for the investigation of a number of serious crimes, including drug trafficking. Turning to Canada, the Controlled Drugs and Substances Act 1996 brought together a range of special powers for the investigation of drug offences and provisions for the confiscation of drug traffickers' assets. As one would expect, these increased powers against suspected drug traffickers have been challenged under the Charter in several cases, and the Supreme Court has made significant rulings. To take three examples; in *Simmons*[30] the Court held that the degree of personal privacy reasonably expected at customs points was lower than elsewhere, and thus upheld various powers of search at the national borders. In *Duarte*,[31] on the other hand, the Court held that electronic surveillance could not be legitimated by obtaining the consent of one of the other participants. In *Silveira*[32] one of the judges, Cory J., called for a legislative code of procedure to deal with the circumstances in which urgent searches may lawfully be made, and the steps that may be taken. As we saw earlier, the Canadian legislature is considering an expansion of investigatory powers in drug trafficking cases.[33] Thus the implication of this small comparative survey is that other countries have thought it necessary to take certain special powers for the investigation of drug trafficking, but that the contentious nature of those powers has been recognised and debated, particularly in Canada.

(iii) Serious fraud:

Is there any justification for adopting special procedures, with reduced safeguards for suspects and defendants, in the investigation of serious fraud? The group who drafted the *Corpus Iuris* were absolutely clear about this:

> The budget, defined as 'the visible sign of a true patrimony common to the citizens of the Union', is the supreme instrument of European policy. To say this emphasises the extreme seriousness of any crime which undermines this patrimony.[34]

From this starting point, the report argues that fraud on the European financial system is complex, hidden, transnational and organised. All of this is taken to support the claim that special measures are required, focussed on simpler and more effective cross-jurisdictional procedures. The report claims adherence to the fundamental rights protected by the Convention and by the European Court of Justice, although that claim may be said to demonstrate the limitations of the Convention. In fact the *Corpus Iuris* proposes the creation of a European Public Prosecutor, with elements of judicial control but no overall accountability for its policies. Whilst the focus of its concern is frauds with cross-border dimensions, the reference to the hidden nature of much fraud strikes a chord with the reasoning behind the domestic legislation which introduced special powers for the investigation of serious fraud. Thus George Staple, writing as Director of the Serious Fraud Office, commented:

the fact is that, faced with the myriad of opportunities for conceal-
ment of fraudulent activities which companies and trusts provide,
Parliament has established an inquisitorial regime in relation to
serious or complex fraud, and has given the SFO the power to call
upon a person to come into the open and to disclose information
which may incriminate him.[35]

These words were written a few years before the Strasbourg
Court held that evidence obtained from the compulsory questioning could not be used in an ensuing prosecution without
violating Article 6 of the Convention[36]; the purpose of including
them here is to identify the reasoning behind the decision to
provide stronger powers. It seems that the ease with which
these offences can be concealed is cited no less frequently than
their intrinsic seriousness when calling for greater powers.

(iv) Special procedures and defendants' rights:

We have noticed that categories such as terrorism and organised
crime are often used in order to introduce extended powers of
intrusion. In the countries surveyed above, it is not the rights in
either Articles 5 or 6 but rather the right to respect for one's
personal life (the so-called privacy right) which is most often
interfered with. Under Article 8 of the European Convention,
interference with the right can be justified on certain grounds,
particularly if it can be shown to be "necessary in a democratic
society" for the prevention of serious crime.[37] In Germany the
Constitutional Court has constructed from the privacy right a
Recht auf informationelle Selbstbestimmung (a right to determine
the use of one's own personal data),[38] and the provision for
intrusive powers to investigate cases of organised crime and
drug trafficking may be regarded as a justifiable exception to
this. Similarly, the extended powers provided in Canada by the
Controlled Drugs and Substances Act 1996 interfere chiefly with
the privacy right. The same trend can be seen in Scandinavian
countries, in respect of what they term "new crimes" (terrorism,
drug trafficking and organised crime). Thus in Norway an Act
amending the Penal Code and Criminal Procedure Code relating to "new investigation methods" was passed in 1999. This
legislation both curtailed some forms of investigation, on the
grounds that they appeared incompatible with the European
Convention, and expanded other forms in a way that was
believed to conform to the Convention. The "new investigation
methods" include secret surveillance, secret searches and sei-
zures, and the use of undercover officers. However, it is
noticeable that this law incorporates several safeguards for the

suspect, not only in terms of the required authorisation procedures, but also by providing for the court to nominate a defence counsel to safeguard the suspect's rights, without making contact with the suspect.[39] If an ordinary adversarial procedure would be inappropriate, then this alternative approach shows clear respect for Convention rights rather than minimalism.

Apart from incursions into privacy, another sphere of special powers is during the trial process. This has occurred in respect of child witnesses in England in, for example, the Youth Justice and Criminal Evidence Act 1999; in France in procedures introduced into the *Code de procédure pénale* by a law of June 17, 1998, Article 28; and in Italy by amendments now located in Article 498 paragraph 4 of the *Codice di Procedura Penale*. Several countries have also brought in laws allowing witnesses to remain anonymous in certain circumstances. This is a controversial step, since (as we saw in Chapter 2B) there are several Strasbourg judgments which hold that witness anonymity may deprive the defendant of a fair trial, even in the rare situations where it can be justified, unless measures are taken to compensate the defendant for the disadvantages he suffers. The Scandinavian countries, which often introduce legislation along similar lines to one another, have fallen into disagreement about the propriety of using anonymous witnesses. Sweden and Denmark have declined to allow them, on the basis that they necessarily restrict the rights of the defence too greatly, whereas Norway has pressed ahead and in 2000 passed an "Act amending the Penal Code and Criminal Procedure Code for the protection of actors in criminal cases against threats and reprisals etc."[40] The Act allows witnesses to remain anonymous only under certain conditions—where the charge is a serious offence connected with organised criminal activity, where anonymity is "strictly necessary", and where that does not entail "significant impairments of the defence", and so on. These safeguards show concern for human rights, even though the debates leading up to the legislation appear to have focused more particularly on the rights of victims of serious crime, and on the imperatives of detecting and preventing organised crime.

In Italy there is no provision for witness anonymity,[41] but there are special circumstances under which the prosecution may be permitted to rely on statements made at an earlier stage and not repeated at trial. Thus when Article 111 of the Italian Constitution was reformulated in 1999 so as to articulate a number of fair trial rights, along the lines of Article 6 of the European Convention, three exceptions to the principle of adversarial proceedings appeared in paragraph 5, the third of which applies to cases where there have been threats against witnesses by the defendant or by a criminal organisation.[42] If the conditions are met, statements made during the *precedemente rese* (preliminary investigation) may be introduced at the trial.[43]

(v) Expanding definitions:

The question of definitions is an important one. Labels have an emotive effect, and in some cases they enlist support simply because few people would wish to be heard opposing such self-evidently righteous initiatives. Who would stand up and declare that there should be no special attempt to prevent organised crime, or to combat terrorism? The emotive sway of these labels makes it particularly important to take a critical view of the definitions employed, and to be on guard against the covert expansion of the categories of case to which they apply. Thus the Terrorism Act 2000 considerably expands the definition of "terrorism" from that to which the previous legislation, chiefly the Prevention of Terrorism (Temporary Provisions) Act 1989, applied. No longer is it limited to terrorism involving the use of violence and putting people in fear. The expanded definition includes serious damage to property, serious risks to the health or safety of the public and serious disruption to electronic systems. Additionally, it is not confined to activities related to Northern Ireland.[44] The Government justified this on the basis that, even if the Northern Ireland problems were to abate, new threats may arise and laws should be in place to deal with them.[45] The Government pointed to "the possibility that some new group or individual could operate in this way in the future, threatening serious violence to people and property."[46] The point here is that the extension of special powers, especially when they run counter to the spirit of human rights, should require far more concrete justification than this. Account should also be taken of the likelihood that these broad powers would be used, within the ample scope of the new definition, on a much wider scale than has been conceded in the official statements.[47]

Similar concerns can be raised about the definition of "organised crime": the images are those of international gangs, or local rackets run by wealthy gangsters, but in practice the activities of small-time cigarette smugglers or handlers of stolen property may well be those targeted under such powers. We have noted that the German law, which provides extended powers of telephone tapping and use of personal data, refers to offences committed in a commercial or habitual manner, and that the French law extending the period of custodial remand, refers to offences committed in an organised group. In both cases the interpretation of the relatively broad concepts is crucial, for they could easily be used in an expansive manner so as to encompass small-time repeat offenders who have a few contacts with other offenders.

The expansion of definitions of key legal concepts would be less of a concern, however, if any special new powers were accompanied by special safeguards for suspects and defendants—along the lines found in various laws in Austria, Norway and Sweden. If appropriate safeguards are introduced, the expansion of definitions is not a way of avoiding rights. However, the trend in this country and some others has been to introduce enhanced powers of surveillance and investigation without going as far as some other European nations to ensure that individual rights are safeguarded. For example, the Regulation of Investigatory Powers Act 2000 allows intrusions on the Article 8 rights of individuals in certain circumstances, without judicial supervision (as required by Convention jurisprudence) and without appointing someone whose task is to ensure that the rights of those subjected to surveillance are properly maintained. The idea of appointing someone for this kind of purpose, adopted in legislation in Norway and in Austria,[48] was not regarded as necessary for these purposes,[49] although it has been adopted subsequently as part of the machinery for challenging the certification of a person as a "suspected international terrorist" under the Anti-terrorism, Crime and Security Act 2001.[50]

The response to some of these proposals is likely to take the form of an assertion that greater powers of investigation and special procedures are necessary on account of the seriousness of these crimes, and that it may be necessary to curtail individual rights in order to protect public interests. It is now time to confront this argument directly.

C. MAKING EXCEPTIONS FOR SERIOUS CRIME?

One basic assumption, sometimes explicit and sometimes implicit, underlying many judicial and political statements is that where the public interests in detecting and prosecuting a crime are high—as with serious crimes—the case for individual rights is weaker. To what extent, if at all, should the safeguards provided by the various Convention rights be affected by the relative seriousness of the crime being investigated? One response to this question is to point out that the Convention rights are minimum guarantees: it may therefore be appropriate to introduce *greater* safeguards in some spheres, but the minimum rights should always be guaranteed, no matter how serious or minor the offence is. This seems to be the position taken by the Committee of Ministers of the Council of Europe in its recommendation on "Crime Policy in Europe in a time of change". Their motivation for examining this subject was the emergence of serious forms of crime in the wake of the great economic and political upheavals of the late 1980s and early 1990s in the states of Eastern Europe. One of the purposes of the recommendation seems to have been to "steady the ship". Thus recommendation 1(a) begins as follows:

> 1. Every response to crime must conform to the basic principles of democratic states governed by the rule of law and subject to the paramount aim of guaranteeing respect for human rights.
> 2. Therefore, however serious the situation of a society might be with respect to crime, any measures aimed at dealing with that situation that do not take account of the values of democracy, human rights and the rule of law are inadmissible.[51]

These recommendations recognise that politicians will be tempted to take strong measures to combat what is perceived as serious crime, if only to be seen to be taking some "firm action", and that human rights will therefore be at risk. This problem is certainly not confined to new states in former communist countries. The provisions of the Anti-terrorism, Crime and Security Act 2001 were the object of considerable criticism from the Joint Committee on Human Rights,[52] and the Government's decision to derogate from Article 5(1) of the Convention (detention without trial of "suspected international terrorists") is certainly open to challenge on the ground that several government statements about the nature of the terrorist threat contradict the assertion that, at the end of 2001, this country was in a state of "public emergency threatening the life of the nation", as Article 15 requires.

We have already seen that declarations such as that of the Council of Europe cannot be taken at face value. The exhortation contained in this recommendation is welcome, but its practical effects will depend on the decisions of Member States to follow the spirit rather than the letter of the recommendation. In policy documents in the United Kingdom, for example, references to Council of Europe recommendations are as rare as a hen's tooth. Moreover, within this recommendation, the references to the rule of law and human rights may be more indeterminate than might appear at first sight. The substance of these safeguards is to be found in the Articles of the European Convention, and we have already noted the varying extent to which the Strasbourg Court and the British courts have seen fit to take account of the seriousness of the crime being investigated when determining the proper interpretation of a Convention right. In Articles 8–11 the seriousness of the crime is clearly a relevant consideration, whereas in Articles 2 and 3 it is not at all relevant. There is considerable debate about its relevance to Articles 5 and 6, although the Strasbourg Court has insisted, in the main, on adherence to the minimum rights guaranteed by the Convention, no matter how serious or minor is the crime being investigated.[53] Some decisions on Article 5 have recognised the need for special measures to combat terrorism, but many decisions (not all) have held that such measures should not be allowed to encroach on the essence of the right. On the other hand, as we saw in part C of the second lecture, British courts have been reluctant to cite these Strasbourg authorities, and have reached decisions which suggest that the protections in Articles 5 and 6 may be diluted,[54] or even overridden,[55] by reference to the serious nature or the minor nature of the crime involved.

Most of these matters were also aired in the report of a Council of Europe seminar on "Serious Crime and Human Rights," from which a strong message can be distilled. Serious crime should indeed be treated seriously, the report affirms, but this should not mean that measures which test or cross the boundaries set by the Convention need to be adopted. A particularly important theme of the report is that a wide variety of alternative techniques are available which do not involve any watering-down of the Convention rights. The primary response should be to deploy a range of civil, regulatory and financial measures to tackle the mischief, and the enactment of new offences with proportionately high penalties should be regarded as a fall-back approach. Enforcement is a key issue, and what one sometimes finds is that an argument is put for exceptional investigatory measures to combat a certain type of offence in circumstances where the relevant enforcement machinery is understaffed and underfunded compared with the "normal" police. What this may mean, in effect, is that governments may want to use the conferment of exceptional powers on investigators in order to conceal their true priorities in enforcement, which lie with the policing of less serious crime. The proper approach to tackling serious crime, as I have argued more fully elsewhere,[56] requires the following steps:

(1) First, decide what crimes are the most serious. This is often thought to be obvious, whereas it is controversial and calls for careful weighing of the interests invaded by certain types of offending. No easy formula presents itself,[57] but some progress can be made by separating threats to the person from threats to property, immediate attacks from remote harms, and more culpable from less culpable wrongs.[58] This process of examining the elements of crimes is essential in the face of expanding and flexible definitions of terrorism and of organised crime.

(2) Secondly, the more serious the interests invaded or threatened by the offence, the stronger the case for criminalising the conduct in addition to relying on civil or regulatory measures.[59]

(3) Thirdly, the more serious the offence, the higher the priority that ought to be given to dealing with it. This requires a range of preventive and other social measures, but it also calls for a re-allocation of resources for enforcement. Resources for this purpose are finite, and so priorities must be reconsidered. Thus, if certain forms of pollution or unsafe transport systems are recognised as involving serious crimes, their enforcement should be given the appropriate priority. It makes little sense to have a "heavy" policing system aimed at low-level crime and disorder, whilst inadequate resources are allocated to the investigation of admittedly more serious offences. At least, this makes no sense as a matter of rational policy.[60] It might make sense to those who treat criminal justice policy as a means of keeping certain sections of the community in check, and of gaining electoral advantage for politicians and their parties.

Only when a government has conscientiously worked through all three steps, I would submit, should it proceed to the question of principle: where a crime is agreed to be especially serious, and where the argument in favour of devoting extra resources to its enforcement and investigation has been accepted, is there a justification for diminishing the safeguards for accused persons and for expanding the powers that may be used against such persons?

A good starting point is to reflect on a lengthy passage from the judgment of Sachs J. in the South African Constitutional Court:

111

Much was made during argument of the importance of combating corporate fraud and other forms of white collar crime. I doubt that the prevalence and seriousness of corporate fraud could itself serve as a factor which could justify reversing the onus of proof. There is a paradox at the heart of all criminal procedure, in that the more serious the crime and the greater the public interest in securing convictions of the guilty, the more important do constitutional protections of the accused become. The starting point of any balancing enquiry where constitutional rights are concerned must be that the public interest in ensuring that innocent people are not convicted and subjected to ignominy and heavy sentences, massively outweighs the public interest in ensuring that a particular criminal is brought to book. Hence the presumption of innocence, which serves not only to protect a particular individual on trial, but to maintain public confidence in the enduring integrity and security of the legal system. Reference to the prevalence and seriousness of a crime therefore does not add anything new or special to the balancing exercise. The perniciousness of the offence is one of the givens, against which the presumption of innocence is pitted from the beginning, not a new element to be put into the scales as part of a justificatory balancing exercise. If this were not so, the ubiquity and ugliness argument could be used in relation to murder, rape, car-jacking, house-breaking, drug-smuggling, corruption . . . the list is unfortunately almost endless, and nothing would be left of the presumption of innocence, save, perhaps, for its relic status as a doughty defender of rights in the most trivial cases.[61]

This passage contains a number of arguments. Its main thrust is the point perhaps most frequently overlooked by politicians and some judges: that where the crime is very serious, there is not only a heightened public interest in ensuring that the guilty are convicted, but the moral injustice done to a person wrongly convicted of such an offence is also heightened. It is surely more important to protect a person from wrongful conviction of a serious crime than from wrongful conviction of a minor crime. Let us examine three of the steps by which Justice Sachs reaches this conclusion.

First, is the wrongful conviction of an innocent person so much more detrimental to the public interest than the acquittal of a guilty person? In his Hamlyn lectures nearly 50 years ago Glanville Williams chronicled the varying ratios in which the common law maxim had been expressed—is it better that five, 10 or even 100 guilty persons should be acquitted rather than one innocent person convicted?[62] The numbers of guilty persons acquitted cannot be a matter of indifference, and this is part of the weakness of this approach to the problem. Clearly, if significant numbers of guilty persons are being acquitted, this may itself threaten "confidence in the legal system", however that might be measured. The purpose of using these ratios of guilty to innocent is, of course, largely rhetorical: it is one means of indicating the importance of adhering to basic safeguards, in terms of procedural requirements, standard of proof and the admissibility of evidence. One necessary precondition is to ascertain that the choice really exists, *i.e.* that a particular rule aimed at safeguarding the innocent would lead to fewer convictions of the guilty—this does not always follow, and may in some cases be avoided by other means. It is also essential to insist that the system gives special weight to the danger of mistaken conviction, and does not simply regard it as being on the same level as a wrongful acquittal. As Antony Duff argues, a mistaken conviction:

> may inflict unnecessary and unpleasant treatment on someone who is in fact harmless; deprive her, needlessly, of the ability to predict and control her own life; and injure her reputation and her prospects, if it leads others to believe mistakenly that she is a law-breaker.[63]

These are all parts of what Dworkin has referred to as the "moral harm" suffered by a person mistakenly convicted—it is the fact of criminal conviction, with its attendant public censure and condemnation, which makes this so deep a wrong. Yet critics will respond that, when a guilty person is acquitted because of a rule of evidence designed to secure the protection of the innocent, this may be no less an injustice to society and to the victim. A three-stage response may be made to this. First, we should recall that much turns on one's conception of victims' rights: in the first lecture it was argued that the victim of an alleged crime should not be accorded any particular rights that alter the agreed rules of a fair trial and sentencing process, except where that is necessary exceptionally to ensure that the victim's rights under the European Convention on Human Rights are respected. Secondly, as for the notion of an injustice to society through an unwarranted acquittal, this is a diffused kind of failure of justice, which does not usually impinge on any individual in the same direct way as a mistaken conviction does.[64] Thirdly, the priority should in principle be to avoid both unjust acquittals and wrongful convictions; but, in the rare cases when it does come down to a choice, we should avoid the direct injustice of a wrongful conviction rather than the diffused injustice of a wrongful acquittal.

The second stage in Justice Sachs' argument is that fundamental rights such as the presumption of innocence must be upheld in order "to maintain public confidence in the enduring integrity and security of the legal system." This is a rather less convincing point, I would suggest. It may be true that public confidence in the courts is especially important to emerging democracies, but it is quite possible that a majority of people would reject such a low rating of the goal of convicting the guilty and would prefer to see measures which are *in*consistent with fundamental or constitutional rights. The difficulty lies in the slippery notion of "public confidence": it is a concept much relied on by judges and politicians, yet it is a concept with an uncertain meaning and with unreliable foundations.[65] The British Crime Survey regularly asks around 10,000 citizens about their confidence in certain criminal justice agencies, such as the courts, the police, the probation service and so forth.[66] This might not meet the point in question, since we are concerned here about particular rights and practices in the investigation, prosecution and trials of accused persons—but then it is possible that more specific questions of this kind could be asked. The problem of unreliable foundations then comes to the fore. If one asks citizens about their confidence in certain procedures, etc., what might be the factual basis for their judgments? Do they know about evidence of the efficacy or otherwise of the procedures? If public attitude surveys about sentencing are a fair indication, then many attitudes expressed would be based on completely erroneous impressions of the prevailing system and its outcomes, not to mention the arguments for and against certain institutional procedures. Some would argue that the foundations of any lack of public confidence do not matter: perceptions are more important than reality.[67] But then policy-makers ought to deal with the perceptions, as such, if there are no corresponding problems in reality. Overall, notions of "public confidence" must surely be seen as an unsatisfactory foundation for the kinds of argument we are dealing with here. Only at the extremes, where there is a danger of a serious loss to the legitimacy of the system because of adverse public attitudes which cannot be dispelled by other means, should policy changes be influenced by unreconstructed "public confidence".

The third stage of Justice Sachs' reasoning is that references to the prevalence and seriousness of the crime add nothing new to the debate, because of the point that the innocent defendant's need for protection rises in proportion to the seriousness of the crime. Moreover, if the seriousness of crime reasoning were allowed full rein, it would tend to undermine the very structure of rule-of-law protections and procedural rights. That is because there are many serious crimes, including murder, manslaughter, rape and so forth—if one were to add prevalent crimes, such as supplying drugs, street robbery or car-jacking, the list would be even longer. What Justice Sachs refers to as "the ubiquity and ugliness argument"—that rights should be curtailed for crimes which are prevalent or serious—really embodies a rejection of the notion of fundamental rights, at least in the kinds of case where those rights are most important to the right-holder. In his view, which is consistent with the general approach of the European Court of Human Rights in relation to almost all aspects of the right to a fair trial except the presumption of innocence (see lecture 2, parts B and C(i) above), the public interest in the investigation and prosecution of serious crimes is not a good reason for compromising on fundamental rights.

A person accused of a serious crime has much more at stake, and therefore deserves no less (indeed, one might argue, more) protection from wrongful conviction.[68] When designing criminal procedures, the aim should be to reserve the most thorough processes for the most serious offences. In English law this has been the primary rationale for the distinction between trial by jury in the Crown Court and summary trial in a magistrates' court. Similarly, the duties of prosecution disclosure are significantly greater for offences tried at the Crown Court than for those tried in the magistrates' courts. Again, it is not unfamiliar in English law to find that the more intrusive investigative measures and other powers are restricted to the more serious forms of crime. Thus, the power of arrest on reasonable suspicion without warrant is confined to "arrestable offences", defined chiefly as those with a maximum penalty of five years or more[69]; longer periods of detention, etc., are also permitted where a person is being questioned in relation to a "serious arrestable offence"[70]; the power to issue a warrant to search private premises is also confined to cases where there are reasonable grounds for believing that a "serious arrestable offence" has been committed[71]; the grant of warrants to intercept communications is limited to cases of "the prevention and detection of serious crime"[72]; and so on.

There is, however, another side to this. Insofar as specially intrusive powers of investigation are thought justifiable for certain types of serious crime, any such powers should be accompanied by equally special safeguards for the innocent. To some extent the Regulation of Investigatory Powers Act 2000 respects this approach, by instituting authorisation procedures which are more demanding as the intrusiveness of the powers increases—although the safeguards in that Act still fall short of requiring the degree of judicial supervision normally insisted upon by the European Court of Human Rights.[73] An example of taking individual rights seriously may be found in an Austrian law of July 10, 1997, which gives the police extraordinary powers of surveillance in order to investigate organised crime, including permission to install recording equipment inside private premises. The procedural safeguards are also strict:

> the exercise of the powers assumes: 1) serious suspicions of an equally serious crime, carrying a sentence of more than 10 years, or an offence of criminal organization; 2) a very serious threat to public order; 3) the necessity of these measures for the investigation of the case; 4) the existence of a criminal procedure which is already underway; 5) the authorization of a committee of three judges from the trial court lasting one month and renewable; and 6) the filing of a report by the officer in charge. An important detail: a civil servant charged with the protection of rights (*Rechtsschutzbeauftrager*), appointed by the Minister of the Interior, must protect the fundamental rights and freedoms of the suspect, and in case of violation, can petition the court of appeals.[74]

This shows how seriously it is possible to take the rights of a person suspected of a grave crime.[75] It demonstrates the value of procedures, notably the appointment of an official as a protector of rights. There is, admittedly, considerable indeterminacy in the procedures—when is an alleged offence a *serious* threat to public order, when are measures *necessary* in the case, etc.—but it is inevitable that the practical success of any procedure will depend on the enthusiasm with which the relevant officials implement it.

Before leaving the relationship of human rights to serious crime, we should also give brief consideration to the reverse argument that, where the crime is minor and has only low penalties, there is less ground for insisting on full respect for human rights. This might seem to chime well with the argument so far, which is that the reasons for upholding the privilege against self-incrimination (set out in lecture 1, part D2) are stronger where the crime is more serious. The converse of this argument probably underlay the decision in *Brown v. Stott*,[76] where the Privy Council held that the compulsion on a car owner to answer questions about who was driving the car at a particular time, on pain of conviction for failing to answer, did not infringe the privilege against self-incrimination which forms part of the right to a fair trial under Article 6. A reconstruction of the Privy Council's reasoning would be that the duty was such an undemanding one, and its importance so great in terms of maintaining a safe road traffic system, that the privilege against self-incrimination should not be applied. Similar reasoning has prevailed in the English courts in relation to the duty to disclose income and assets to the tax authorities.[77] If one applies Dworkinian analysis to this,[78] then perhaps one would invoke his third possible justification for allowing the public interest to override a basic right *in extremis*—that is, the argument that the assault on the car owner's dignity, by forcing her or him to answer a possibly self-incriminating question, is relatively slight (and, presumably, the penalty for non-compliance so low) in comparison with the great social cost, in terms of road safety and casualty rates, of maintaining that car owners have no duty to answer such questions. The suggestion here is simply that Dworkinian reasoning might in principle accommodate the notion that fewer protections are required for minor offences which make only minor incursions into basic rights. It is not being suggested that the argument necessarily applies so as to support *Brown v. Stott*, since there are significant issues still to be discussed—was the penalty for non-compliance so low?[79] Would the abolition of the statutory duty to give information result, necessarily or even probably, in reduced road safety and higher casualties? Could other measures be taken which, without infringing fundamental rights, would minimise or eliminate the social cost? It is essential that these more empirical issues are examined, rather than suppressed beneath high-sounding phrases about public safety, if this line of justification is to be persuasive.

Assuming that the necessary empirical questions receive acceptable answers, the question of principle remains. Is there any objection to lowering human rights protections when, to put it bluntly, the stakes are lower in terms of the extent of the citizen's duty and the potential penalty for non-compliance is low? One answer to this would be to draw distinctions among rights, even within the overall Article 6 right to a fair trial. Certain rights would be absolute, such as the right to a hearing before an independent and impartial tribunal, the right to have adequate time and facilities to prepare a defence, and probably several others. There might, however, be some rights—perhaps the privilege against self-incrimination and the presumption of innocence (as applied to reverse burdens of proof)—to which limited exceptions might be contemplated for minor offences. There is some support for this in *Salabiaku v. France*,[80] where the Court held that the presumption of innocence in Article 6(2) did not prohibit reverse onus provisions but required courts to have regard to "what was at stake" in deciding whether they are acceptable; but the reasoning in that judgment is so unconvincing that I would not wish to place great reliance on it, and basic standards ought only to be relaxed where there is no significant stigma attaching to conviction. However, even among human rights advocates there are those who would contend that principles such as the privilege against self-incrimination should not be available to citizens in the context of "a regulatory system to which they have voluntarily subjected themselves": the argument is that "a society is entitled to impose a condition of co-operation with a regulatory regime, backed by criminal sanction. People are free to take it or leave it."[81] Whether this can fairly be applied to motoring is a moot point, but underlying this argument seems to be a belief that such a minor inroad into a cherished right is reasonable, and may help to preserve the strength of the right in more major cases.

A second and stronger argument, running in the opposite direction, is that fundamental rights should be maintained for all criminal offences. This is the approach chiefly advocated by the Strasbourg Court, which has repeatedly held that:

> the general requirements of fairness in Article 6, including the right not to incriminate oneself, apply to criminal proceedings in respect of all types of criminal offences without distinction, from the most simple to the most complex.[82]

On this view, if a domestic legislature does not wish those requirements to apply, it should adopt a "civil law" approach to the issue, or at least resort to some lesser category such as regulations or administrative violations (where both penalties and safeguards may properly be lower).[83] English law does not have any such lesser category of offences at present: it does contain many criminal offences for which liability is strict, and there is evidence that, after a lengthy period of confusion, the English courts are now adopting a more principled approach against strict liability for crimes which carry the possibility of a prison sentence.[84] Nevertheless, there remains the problem that many strict liability offences which have only fines as penalties remain criminal offences, subject to all the normal procedural requirements. It would be possible to transfer some of them into a new, lesser category. So long as the boundary between criminal and civil liability is properly policed, as the Strasbourg Court has endeavoured to do by reaching adverse decisions against several countries which have tried to circumvent the Convention by this means,[85] a "civil law" or regulatory approach should be given careful consideration. This would leave intact the application of fundamental rights to all prohibitions or duties deemed sufficiently important to warrant a criminal sanction.

D. THE "NO RIGHTS WITHOUT RESPONSIBILITIES" THESIS

Many public officials, including the Home Secretary who piloted the Human Rights Act through the House of Commons,[86] have argued that it is necessary to create a human rights culture as well as to pass legislation on the matter. At a minimum, this seems to mean that, as Mr Blair has put it, people working "in public service [must] respect human rights in everything we do."[87] The Lord Chancellor has gone further, claiming that the 1998 Act "will create a more explicitly moral approach to decisions and decision-making."[88] It is not clear what significance attaches to the term "moral" in this context: legal decisions often involve moral arguments, whether explicit or implicit. There is no single morality, of course, and so any reference to moral arguments is really a reference to a style of reasoning and debate, and therefore perhaps to a more open-ended set of arguments than is normally to be found in court judgments. On the other hand, the use of the word "moral" may have been an attempt to distract attention from the claim that the decisions of judges under the Human Rights Act are essentially political or, better, even more political than the general run of their decisions.

This is not the place for a discussion of the character of judicial decision-making, but it is relevant to consider what it means to foster a "human rights culture". For the meaning of "culture" in this context, we may turn to the former Home Secretary Jack Straw, who proposed that "culture" should mean "the habits of mind, the intellectual reflexes and the professional sensibilities which are historically ingrained and typical of the behaviour of a particular group of people."[89] What, then of a "human rights culture"? One might think it means a culture of respect for human rights, an attitude which makes it automatic to think about the human rights implications of decisions and actions, and an attitude which regards the European Convention as a valuable statement of minimum standards rather than as an inconvenient obstacle to be circumvented. This does not require commitment to the notion of "inalienable rights",[90] but it does call upon officials and other citizens to regard the Convention as a form of higher law, which has a special claim on our attention and a special weight in arguments. A healthy human rights culture, it may be argued, is one that recognises the room for argument that human rights documents leave. In the Convention, as we have noted, there are three levels of rights: some, like Articles 2, 3, 4 and 7, have the highest importance because they are non-derogable; others, such as Articles 5 and 6, should be regarded as strong, but they are derogable in limited and extreme circumstances such as war and civil disturbance; and then there is the range of qualified rights in Articles 8–11. In respect of rights falling in the last two categories there will inevitably be controversy, but this is a good thing because there are important issues that need to be addressed as widely as possible. As Tom Campbell has contended, one advantage of the Human Rights Act may be to enable British people to see:

> human rights as a vital part of a culture of controversy in which neither parliaments, courts or the people are to be trusted, and in which the core of politics must be oriented to reaching a series of legally enforceable but temporary agreements as to the rights which best protect and enhance the equal interests of all citizens.[91]

Now this position is probably more open-ended than that espoused by many who have invoked the phrase "human rights culture", but it is none the worse for that. Its merits lie in its acknowledgement that there are indeterminacies which must be resolved, that these are often vital political decisions, and that the concept of human rights has a distinct role to play in the relevant discourse and argumentation.

It seems doubtful, however, whether the Government that introduced the Human Rights Act adopted either of these interpretations of a "human rights culture"—not the idea of human rights as having the special weight of moral minimum standards, nor the notion of human rights as a catalyst for ongoing controversies about the adjustment between individual interests and public interests. Many of the statements by government ministers propounded the idea that human rights go hand in hand with social responsibilities, and that the process of encouraging respect for human rights should also be a process of fostering the recognition of social obligations. A particular passage in Jack Straw's third reading speech in the House of Commons puts this point:

> Over time, the Bill will bring about the creation of a human rights culture in Britain. In future years, historians may regard the Bill as one of the most important measures of this Parliament. I talk about a human rights culture. One of the problems which has arisen in Britain in recent years is that people have failed to understand from where rights come. The philosopher David Selbourne has commented on the generation of an idea of dutiless rights, where people see rights as consumer products which they can take, but for nothing. The truth is that rights have to be offset by responsibilities

and obligations. There can and should be no rights without responsibilities, and our responsibilities should precede our rights. In developing that human rights culture, I want to see developed a much clearer understanding among Britain's people and institutions that rights and responsibilities have properly to be balanced— freedoms by obligations and duties . . .[92]

This is a position which accepts the critique that much "rights-talk" is excessively individualistic and that it tends to portray individuals as detached from the community in which they live, a community in which, inevitably, both benefits and burdens fall on to each member.[93] Thus, as Mr Straw stated on another occasion:

> The culture of rights and responsibilities we need to build is not about giving the citizen a new cudgel with which to beat the State. That's the old-fashioned libertarian idea that gave the whole rights movement a bad and selfish name. The idea that forgot that rights don't exist in a vacuum, that forgot the relationship between the individual and the group. That's not the culture of rights and responsibilities we want or need.[94]

This serves to confirm that the "rights culture" of which Mr Straw and other government ministers spoke is properly described as a "culture of rights and responsibilities", but it also suggests that this broad notion is applied to Articles 5 and 6 as much as to the rights declared in other Articles. Indeed, Mr Straw specifically mentioned Article 6 in his discussion of how rights must be balanced against other rights, although his only example was the important but unusual decision in *Doorson v. Netherlands*.[95] It seems likely, however, that Mr Straw adopted the same undifferentiated approach to the Convention which has been pursued by some judges since the implementation of the Human Rights Act, to the effect that *any* Convention right can be balanced against public interests when determining whether it applies in a given situation.[96]

What, then, should be said about the coupling of rights to responsibilities?[97] This is not the place for a general debate on the Selbourne approach of deriving rights from duties.[98] In any event, one interpretation of the Government approach articulated by Mr Straw is simply that the Convention includes both rights and duties, because every individual protected by the Convention has the duty to respect the rights of every other individual. There is no difficulty in accepting this proposition, but it is important to tie down its precise relevance for the procedural protections which are the focus of discussion here. In relation to Articles 5, 6 and 7 on fair criminal procedures, surely, the idea of rights either deriving from citizens' responsibilities or being somehow dependent on those responsibilities is a relatively weak one: irrespective of the origins, social status or background of the person charged with a criminal offence, he or she ought to be entitled to certain basic rights—both negative rights not to be detained unreasonably without being brought before a court and not to be forced to incriminate himself, and positive rights to legal assistance, to an interpreter (where necessary), and so on. These are rights which any nation state has a duty to provide: the whole thrust of Article 5 and 6 lies in the belief that the acts of State officials in connection with arrest, charge, detention and other aspects of the criminal process must be in accordance with basic standards and also subject to supervision. Whatever the merits of the Selbourne–Straw approach in relation to rights such as freedom of expression, freedom of religion, respect for privacy and freedom of association, they have little purchase in the context of criminal procedure rights.

This, however, is not the only way in which Mr Straw sought to develop his "no rights without responsibilities" thesis. Another may be traced back to writers such as Amitai Etzioni: here, the concern is not to argue that rights *derive from* citizens' duties, but rather that declarations of rights must be accompanied by a recognition of the need to place limitations on the protection of rights if we are to move towards a safe and well-balanced community.[99] This is a rather curious use of the concept of "responsibility", since what Etzioni has in mind is the introduction of requirements to carry an identity card, or to submit to DNA or drug tests, and other impositions that can be justified by reference to the suppression of crime and the promotion of public safety. Etzioni does not contemplate these incursions on rights lightly, and propounds restrictive criteria that resonate with those developed under the European Convention—that any limitations of rights must be necessary to prevent a clear and present danger, must be necessary in the sense that no less intrusive means will suffice, and must involve the minimum possible incursion on the right. When it comes to justifying these restrictions on rights, he devotes much discussion to his brand of communitarianism, and one of his principal arguments appears to be a form of political pragmatism—that if rights are not "balanced" with responsibilities (*i.e.* restrictions justified on wider social grounds), there would be a danger that the whole notion of fundamental rights might be overthrown by a populist backlash with authoritarian tendencies. That would be such a disastrous result that it would be prudent of rights advocates to seek to pre-empt such an overthrow by making early concessions. Etzioni regards this as a political calculation, but it seems to be a calculation done by someone with little respect for rights, and influenced by a prediction of doom which a human rights advocate should endeavour to falsify rather than to concede.

A more extreme version of communitarian approaches to rights may be found in some of the Asian countries which regard the Western idea of rights as question-begging and even unnecessarily destructive, and some of whose supporters claim that the discourse of human rights conceals a kind of cultural imperialism. The 1990s saw the notion of "Asian values" being developed in Malaysia, Singapore, Indonesia and elsewhere as a means of contradicting the universalism assumed by human rights discourse.[100] Thus the Attorney-General of Singapore argued vigorously against the "Western" view of the bearing of "human rights" on the criminal process. He stated that "the existence of fundamental rights for suspects and accused persons is not in question. It is the scope of such rights that is in issue."[101] Thus the right to a fair trial is accepted, but the view is taken that inroads into the privilege against self-incrimination, adverse inferences from silence and the reversal of the burden of proof may all be justified if the public interest requires them. In these circumstances trials are fair, because they give proper weight to the interests of the community at large. A more vigorous pursuit of human rights, such as that developed by the Strasbourg Court under the European Convention, is opposed because of its probable effects on the whole ethos of the country. Thus the Attorney-General makes much of the effect of the death penalty and corporal punishment, and of the various restrictions mentioned above, in reducing the crime rate in Singapore, in heightening public perceptions that it is a safe country in which to live, and in bolstering economic prosperity.[102] These results are linked back to human rights:

> We should not be apologetic or defensive about a criminal justice system that is effective in reducing the incidence of crime in society. Fewer crimes mean more freedom for all. Individual rights are only meaningful in the context of an established social order. Without society, personal freedom and rights are meaningless.[103]

This is a stark inversion of the human rights approach. It sides unambiguously with State authorities and with the powerful, and fails to insist that the exercise of authority in relation to individuals should be limited and accountable. Crime control is vaunted as the primary objective, and respect for rights is only accepted insofar as it does not interfere with that goal. In effect, there are no rights that can be called "trumps", merely residual areas of liberty over which the State does not wish to make claims. The "Asian values" approach carries considerable social implications for the powerless: given the social circumstances of most of those accused of crime by the law enforcement agencies, these extensive qualifications of human rights represent telling inroads into basic standards and safeguards.

If the "no rights without responsibilities" thesis is to be pursued further, despite the counter-arguments just considered, one might consider what terms might be found in an implied social contract. The issue is acutely contentious, but on the one hand there might be the citizens' duties to pay taxes, avoid using force, obey laws, etc., and on the other hand there might be the State's duty to respect individual rights and to provide support through a welfare system. For a government to pro-claim the Human Rights Act as a milestone in constitutional reform is one thing; for it to join in the criticisms of rights-talk as individualistic and to promote the idea of responsibilities so vigorously, without making significant progress in the vital spheres of social policy that provide an essential grounding for wider human development, is to put the cart before the horse. We must recall that the United Kingdom has one of the highest rates of violation found by the Strasbourg Court—some 50 violations by 1997, and some 30 more since then. Moreover, individual rights of the kind set out in the Convention must be supplemented by recognition of a range of social and economic rights. The European Union's Charter of Fundamental Rights, declared in 2000, is a document that declares a range of political, social, economic and other rights: to what extent it will have political effectiveness remains to be seen, and in the short term it might have little more influence than as a guide to judges in the European Court of Justice.[104] All that we have in our domestic law is what Lord Cooke rightly described as "the rather elderly European Convention."[105] However, that does contain, in Articles 5, 6 and 7, a number of fundamental rights relevant to criminal procedure. These are essentially individu-alistic, and therefore the "no rights without responsibilities" thesis should have no application in this sphere.

E. RIGHTS AND RISK

Much public policy discourse, both in criminal justice and more generally, is connected with the risk society. In terms of serious crime, it is questionable whether the Government's mantras about rights and responsibility are not properly translated as rights and risk. Malcolm Feeley and Jonathan Simon write that "it is now possible to contend that we live in a risk society in which the demand for knowledge useful in risk definition, assessment, management and distribution is refiguring social organisation."[106] Thus, they argue that:

> Threats and dangers, and fears about them, are dealt with by the construction of 'suitable enemies' and attendant negative labelling, denial, avoidance and exclusion. Solidarity is based on a communality of fear. In some cases, such as the 'war on drugs', insecurities are cultivated and focused on unfortunate people to gain political purchase and to offset the endemic insecurity experienced more generally in everyday life.[107]

In a context in which (as we have seen) public interest arguments are being urged by way of exceptions to, or detractions from, the human rights declared, these risk arguments must be scrutinised with care. It is certainly right that social policies should take account of dangerous risks, but there is a tendency of rhetoric to run ahead of proper assessment. One important question is whether the risks at which a policy is aimed are actually as bad as claimed: empirical research has often shown that risks are systematically over-estimated.[108] Another relevant question is whether there are greater risks that are not receiving similar attention.[109] Then there is the more specific question of whether the measures being taken or proposed are effective in dealing with the risk, or are actually able to make only a slight contribution (and are more about fear reduction, which can and ought to be tackled in a less intrusive way). This last point may be illustrated by reference to Government proposals for "progression" in the sentencing of persistent offenders: the policy is trumpeted as if it would constitute a major contribution to public safety, whereas history suggests that such measures often misfire and fail to make a real impression on the "serious persistent offenders" who are the target of the policy, and even the recent Halliday Report records doubts about the incapacitative and deterrent effects of increased severity.[110]

At this stage we must remind ourselves of the point made in the final part of the first lecture: the only reasonable conclusion from the crime figures of the last 10 years is that there has been an increase in serious crimes involving violence and sexual assault. This means that there is greater risk (although it is fair to add that the risk of becoming the victim of such a serious crime remains very low), and that there is at least some basis for public concern. However, there should also be concern about the way that governments play upon the increased risk and propose policies that are unlikely to be effective but which have some prospects of bringing politicial success. In criminal procedure, as in sentencing, the easy populist route leads to the promotion of "a punitive 'law and order' stance" designed to "restore public confidence", yet which "routinely den[ies] limitations that are acknowledged by their own administrations" (*i.e.* by the research arms of the very departments which put the policies forward).[111] As Andrew von Hirsch argues:

> If 'law and order' measures lack apparent substantive goals of justice or crime prevention, and cater mostly to resentment, are their advocates being irrational? They are not. The strategies have an instrumental function, but it is not primarily a substantive one: it is concerned, instead, with the acquisition of power. Exploiting popular resentment is a way—and, sometimes, unhappily, an effective way—of garnering political support.[112]

It is not merely, therefore, that many judges and politicians seem to be willing to give preference to "public interest" arguments over fundamental rights, but also that some of the "public interest" arguments owe more to fear than to risk, and more to political posturing than to evidence-based policy selection.

F. FINDING THE RIGHT BALANCE

The discussion in the preceding section serves to re-emphasise a point that has been with us since the beginning of these lectures: that serious crimes are a threat to our safety and security, and it is important that the Government should take measures against it. What we should insist upon, however, is that the empirical foundations of the threat are presented clearly, so as to avoid the tendency to exaggerate for political or other purposes; that the need for any proposed measures of enforcement and investigation is documented, so that people can judge the prospects of those measures being effective (rather than being mere political posturing, or playing on people's fears for their safety); and that human rights protections are not lost in the increase of official powers, and are counterbalanced by additional safeguards.

What should these human rights protections be? These lectures have been confined to rights in criminal proceedings under Articles 5 and 6 of the Convention. In the first lecture I argued that, when the Human Rights Act was being introduced, there was inadequate public or even professional discussion of the nature of the particular rights covered by the Convention. I sketched some reasons for and against 10 possible rights, nine of which are already protected by Article 5 and 6; I did so in the belief that even rights which are declared to be fundamental must be the subject of constant appraisal and re-appraisal. The European Convention dates from 1950, but the Court has shown a willingness to develop the text by implying certain rights in criminal cases. Reflection on the reach of the Convention should not be confined to the Strasbourg judges, and in section G below I urge further discussion of which rights we should treat as fundamental.

A large part of the second lecture was given over to an examination of the judicial approach to conflicts between fundamental rights and the claims of governments for extra powers to deal with serious crime. We saw that the prevailing approach in the Strasbourg Court is to maintain that the essence of the rights under Articles 5 and 6 must be preserved, no matter how serious the crime(s) of which the individual stands accused. On the other hand the British courts, and most particularly the English judiciary, have given rein to a broad notion of "balancing" (which has little support in the Strasbourg jurisprudence on Articles 5 and 6), and on several occasions have held that a fundamental right under Article 5 or 6 should give way to pressing "public interest" considerations. The courts have done this in the name of "proportionality", a notion with an apparent "common sense" appeal but which has the capacity (used as the British courts use it) of making substantial inroads into rights regarded as fundamental. In the second lecture I argued that the British approach is not merely doubtful under the Human Rights Act and erroneous as an application of the European Convention but also unconvincing at the level of principle, in the sense that it fails to respect the nature of rights as protections for individuals against the will of the majority. Earlier in this lecture I took up the theme again, arguing that just as governments may justifiably call for greater powers of enforcement and investigation in respect of serious crimes, so there is an equally strong case for maintaining the fundamental rights of the individual who is suspected or accused of a serious crime. This corollary is too frequently overlooked in this country.

In making the case for the protection of fundamental rights I am not taking my aim solely at the British judiciary, not even against all judges. It behoves Parliament to take the lead in ensuring that rights it has declared to be fundamental are properly upheld in legislation. In practice, that means that the government of the day must "mainstream" human rights (to adopt the current jargon), that is, it must ensure that human rights thinking pervades all policy decisions and proposals for legislation. Marlti Koskenniemi has written persuasively about "the banal administrative recourse to rights language in order to buttress one's political priorities" in contemporary Europe[113] but it seems that British politics has not even reached that stage. In the second lecture I showed how this Government has come forward with some legislative proposals that sail close to the wind, in human rights terms, and others which are only doubtfully compliant. A perusal of the reports of the Joint Committee on Human Rights supports this assessment.[114] The Government proclaimed its desire to foster a "human rights culture", but it then transpired that in the realm of criminal proceedings this was a minimalist commitment. There is more than enough evidence of this in legislation such as the Regulation of Investigatory Powers Act 2000 and in proposals such as the Dangerous People with Severe Personality Disorder Bill. Some of the wide powers that the Government originally tried to take for itself under the Anti-Terrorism, Crime and Security Bill 2001 showed a contempt for human rights, and the statute as enacted is accompanied by a derogation (of doubtful validity) from the Convention. Moreover, as I showed earlier in this lecture, Government ministers muddied the waters by insisting that rights go together with responsibilities—without specifying exactly what that means. Certainly it is everyone's duty to respect the rights of others, and in that sense we all have duties as well as rights. But I argued that if the message is intended to weaken the protections for suspects and defendants under Articles 5 and 6 of the Convention, it is absolutely unsustainable. Those rights attach to people *because* they are suspected or accused of a crime, and there can be no suggestion that their previous (alleged) conduct should determine the extent to which their rights are protected.

It must be recognised, however, that there are a few small pockets of Articles 5 and 6 where the Strasbourg Court has stated either that a particular right is not absolute, or that it may be necessary to balance a right against some other interest. Now this proposition must be treated with care—far more care, I regret to say, than most English judges and politicians have devoted to it. Thus the Strasbourg Court has said that both the right of silence and the privilege against self-incrimination are not absolute,[115] but that emphatically does not mean that they can be freely "balanced" against public interest considerations.

What it means in respect of the right of silence is that there may be "situations calling for an explanation from" the accused, in which adverse inferences may justifiably be drawn from the accused's silence: this is a significant qualification, but we noted that it refers to the evidential situation, and not at all to the seriousness of the crime charged or the complexity of the investigation. It is possible that the Strasbourg Court will modify its approach slightly in the future, and will allow limited exceptions to the privilege against self-incrimination in respect of relatively minor offences which are central to the maintenance of the infrastructure of the community (such as road safety, and the taxation system)[116]; but its present case law does not support any such exception.

As for balancing an Article 6 right against another interest, the principal example of this in recent years is *Doorson v. Netherlands*,[117] where the Court held that the defendant's right to examine witnesses against him has to be balanced against the rights of the witnesses themselves, notably where a witness has reason to fear violent reprisals if her or his identity is revealed. This decision should not be cited without also mentioning that the interests "balanced" were both rights of individuals, not any public interests, and that the process of "balancing" was quite rigidly structured. Thus the Court insisted that, although it was proper to protect the identity of the witness, the rights of the defence must be curtailed as little as possible; the "handicaps under which the defence laboured [must be] sufficiently counterbalanced by the procedures followed by the judicial authorities", such as appropriate directions from the judge; and that any conviction should not be based "solely or mainly" on the evidence of the anonymous witnesses.[118]

A similarly structured approach may be found in the Court's judgments on the prosecution's duty to disclose documents to the defence, and the claim of "public interest immunity" from having to disclose certain evidence. In the leading decision of *Rowe and Davis v. United Kingdom*[119] the Court held that the principle of equality of arms is a requirement of fairness under Article 6, but that:

> the entitlement to disclosure of relevant evidence is not an absolute right. In any criminal proceedings there may be competing interests, such as national security or the need to protect witnesses at risk of reprisals or keep secret police methods of investigating crime. In some cases it may be necessary to withhold certain evidence from the defence so as to preserve the fundamental rights of another individual or to safeguard an important public interest. However, only such measures restricting the rights of the defence which are strictly

necessary are permissible under Article 6(1). Moreover, in order to ensure that the accused receives a fair trial, any difficulties caused to the defence by a limitation on its rights must be sufficiently counter-balanced by the procedures followed by the judicial authorities.[120]

There may be room for debate about whether the Court has insisted on sufficient "counterbalancing" procedures in these cases of public interest immunity,[121] but what is clear is that the reasoning must be structured, and that this lies some distance from the broad balancing in which English courts have some-times indulged—even though two of the three "competing interests" are public interests. Thus, on the rare occasions when the Strasbourg Court has recognised that a degree of balancing may enter into the determination of rights under Articles 5 and 6, it has insisted on structured reasoning. If English courts and politicians are to continue to adopt the metaphor of "balanc-ing", it is submitted that they should at least move to a more rigorous and structured approach. As argued earlier, even the justifications for interfering with the qualified rights under Articles 8–11 of the Convention must be reasoned according to a particular structure of requirements: this renders all the more cogent the argument that rigorous and structured reasoning should be used when there is a question of "balancing" a right under Article 5 or 6 against some public interests.

Am I vaunting the Strasbourg approach unjustifiably? After all, there is no sign in Convention jurisprudence of a "meta-principle to guide rational choice",[122] and so courts and govern-ments will inevitably have considerable leeway in determining the answers to the structured questions. However, the notion of a "meta-principle" might be thought illusory since, even if there were an overriding principle of respect for human dignity, as in the German constitution, its meaning when applied to different situations can only be developed and adjusted in a particularis-tic fashion. It may develop a core meaning, but its application will invariably raise further questions and require further eval-uations. The Strasbourg approach, as it is, also leaves consider-able flexibility to the Court in the interpretation and development of the various Articles, but there appears to be less discretion than is manifest in the broad balancing approach of some English judges. The metaphor of balancing suggests some kind of judicious procedure by which items with a particular weight are put into the scales with other items of a certain weight, so as to determine on which side the greater combined weight is found. We can then have confidence in the objectivity of the solution. But a British court or politician claiming that all the relevant interests have been weighed properly so as to produce a "balanced" solution is confronted with formidable difficulties, since there is usually no explicit discussion of the amount of weight assigned to the various items being balanced, let alone the reasons for thus evaluating them. Nor is there any analysis of the structure of the Convention, and the varying strength of the rights declared therein. All these difficulties are routinely ignored, and there is rarely any openness about the problems of assigning weight to various interests and of assessing combined weights on the two sides of "the scales".

The Strasbourg approach to Articles 5 and 6, in treating certain rights as fundamental, and in accepting that they can be curtailed only on certain strict conditions, is clearly superior. As argued in the second lecture, this is a triangulated approach which takes account of the right itself, the public interest considerations, and compensating safeguards in the event of some restriction on the right; in this respect, too, it differs from the British approach which, it seems, finds little place for that third element. The strength of the Strasbourg approach is to specify procedures for determining the difficult issues, articulating the public interest considerations, identifying the essence of the right, and looking into the provision of safeguards. It ought therefore to be less opaque, but of course there remains considerable indeterminacy. Procedures take one a certain distance, but they cannot conceal the need for value judgments to be made by politicians or by courts. On what basis should they take decisions about whether certain public interests are sufficiently strong to justify curtailing a right? Some would argue that the meta-principle should be the republican ideal of liberty: the difficult clashes between individual rights and public interests should be resolved by calculating which approach advances "dominion" on a greater scale—dominion meaning non-interference by others, secured by society and the community so as to become the expectation of each individual.[123] The difficulty in accepting such consequentialist formulae[124] is that they do not assign any priority or special weight to human rights as such, and seem not to recognise the concept of rights as claims against the majority will. Balancing is to take place, but it does not appear that any particular rights are to be treated as prioritised, as the notion of fundamental rights requires. It is therefore not clear why the public interests should not prevail every time.

My own preference would be to admit that human rights standards have areas of open texture, in which policy choices have to be made both by legislatures and by judges. Criticisms of the indeterminacy of human rights standards must be brushed aside: all legal standards are more or less indeterminate, and that should focus our attention on the exercise of the power to interpret and develop those standards. To a certain extent I would follow Tom Campbell[125] in recognising that fundamental rights should form part of the essential dialogue of politics, what he refers to as a "culture of controversy". This should draw legal and political arguments closer together, recognising that reasoning about human rights and public interests cannot be exclusively legal or exclusively political.[126] But I would insist that human rights be given some priority over majoritarian wishes and interests, and this is why I would not accept any balancing approach that does not recognise that Articles 5 and 6 are, in Dworkin's memorable term, "trumps" over public interest considerations. There may be situations in which a limited amount of "over-trumping" is rightly allowed, but by their nature these must be extreme and urgent cases, and never frequent or normal; and the Strasbourg Court's doctrine that the "essence" of the rights should not be destroyed is worth maintaining and refining. Any such over-trumping should be decided only after a transparent analysis of the allegedly pressing public interests, following the kind of procedure that the Strasbourg Court has required.[127] Where any curtailment is approved, it should be counter-balanced by safeguards of the kind described above, including an adversarial procedure for challenge or, if necessary, the appointment of special counsel to represent a defendant's interests. One of the great achievements of the Strasbourg Court, in my view, has been its development of, and insistence upon, this kind of procedural approach to difficult human rights issues.

G. THE FUTURE OF FUNDAMENTAL RIGHTS

Throughout this discussion of the interaction of human rights, serious crime and criminal procedure, I have emphasised what I see as the consequences of classifying a right as fundamental. However, I have also sought to encourage debate over the contents of the category of fundamental rights: in the first lecture I lamented the dearth of public and professional discussion about the contents of the particular rights at the time when the Human Rights Bill was going through Parliament, and in the second lecture I raised questions about what "fair trial" rights should or should not be classified as fundamental. As one who does not regard human rights as inherent in the human condition or as unchanging, I welcome re-appraisal of the claims of the various rights now expressed or implied into Article 6. Is the privilege against self-incrimination worthy of its status as a fundamental right? Should exceptions be made to it? Is the presumption of innocence worth preserving in its present form? If so, should it not be taken more seriously, and exceptions scrutinised with greater care? Does the right to legal aid and assistance in Article 6(3) go far enough?

This re-appraisal ought to extend to considering the claims of other rights to be given the status of "fundamental rights". A recent example of this is to be found in Protocol 7, Article 4, which introduced into the Convention the "right not to be tried or punished twice" (discussed in the first lecture, part D10). Other candidates are the right not to be subjected to disproportionate punishment, for which there is scattered recognition but no clear statement[128]; the right not to be subjected to criminal conviction without proof of fault (or, at least, not to be imprisoned for a criminal offence without proof of fault); and a number of rights connected with methods of investigation and interrogation, including the use of deception. Issues of this kind must be brought into the mainstream of human rights discussion: democratic processes ought to, as it were, take them back from the judicial fora in which they too frequently rest. Public and professional debate about the recognition and contents of basic rights is vital if the European Convention is not to become disastrously cut off from the democratic countries that are subject to it, or to become so remote from the issues affecting criminal investigation that its precepts are no longer recognised as truly fundamental.

---

[1] Although that has happened in the aftermath of the events of September 11, 2001, in relation to anti-terrorism measures. See the Home Secretary, David Blunkett, reported in *The Times*, September 24, 2001, p.1, who "warned Labour backbenchers worried about the possible violation of human rights that failure to act would allow terrorists to 'make a monkey out of us'", and subsequently proposed a derogation from Art. 5 to allow the detention without trial of certain foreign nationals, a derogation that has now taken effect under the Anti-Terrorism, Crime and Security Act 2001.

[2] (1996) 22 E.H.R.R. 293.

[3] A draft bill, put out for comment by the Home Secretary, will consolidate and expand these confiscation powers: Proceeds of Crime Bill 2001.

[4] *Phillips v. U.K.*, judgment of July 5, 2001; the dissenting judges make a powerful case for regarding the procedure as criminal, even though they did not differ as to the result of the case. See also *Benjafield* [2001] 2 Cr.App.R. 7.

[5] The Labour Party, *A Quiet Life* (1995).

[6] See the discussion of *Brogan v. U.K.* and other decisions in Chap. 2.

[7] I am grateful to Caroline Fennell and her unpublished doctoral thesis for these perspectives.

[8] (1996) 22 E.H.R.R. 330; see above, pp. 33–35.
[9] For discussion and further references, see D. Hobbs, "Criminal Collaboration", in M. Maguire, R. Morgan and R. Reiner (eds.), *Oxford Handbook of Criminology* (2nd ed., Oxford U.P., 1997), pp 822–832.
[10] U.N. Convention news-sheet, "After Palermo: an Overview of what the Convention and Protocols hope to accomplish", www.odccp.org/palermo/sum1.html.
[11] United Nations, *United Nations Convention against Transnational Organized Crime* (2000), Art. 20.1.
[12] Council of Europe, Recommendation No. R(96) 8, *Crime Policy in Europe in a time of Change*; see also V. Mitsilegas, "Defining organised crime in the European Union", (2001) 26 E.L.Rev. 565.
[13] (1999) 133 C.C.C. (3d) 257.
[14] Sections 98a and 100a, discussed below, p. 103.
[15] C. Bassiouni, "Criminalité organisée et terrorisme: pour une stratégie d'interventions efficaces", *Indice Pénale*, 1990, pp. 5–6.
[16] M. Pieth, "The Prevention of Money-Laundering: a Comparative Analysis", (1998) 6 *E.J. of Crime, Criminal Law and Criminal Justice* 159, p. 161. In the Anti-terrorism, Crime and Security Act 2001, Pt 1 and Sched. 1 extend the power for forfeiture of "terrorist cash", and Pt 2 and Sched. 3 extend the powers to make "freezing orders".
[17] In *Gilligan v. Criminal Assets Bureau* [1998] 3 I.R. 185.
[18] (1995) 20 E.H.R.R. 247, at para. 36; see also *Phillips v. U.K.* [2001] Crim.L.R. 817.
[19] *Phillips v. U.K.*, *ibid.*; *cf.* the general survey by J. Pradel, "The Criminal Justice Systems facing the Challenge of Organized Crime", 69 *Revue Internationale de Droit Penal* 673, pp. 678–679.
[20] Joint Committee on Human Rights, Eleventh Report, Session 2001–2002: *Proceeds of Crime Bill* (2002).
[21] See, *e.g.*, D. Hobbs, "Criminal Collaboration", in M. Maguire, R. Morgan and R. Reiner (eds), *Oxford Handbook of Criminology* (2nd ed., Oxford U.P., 1997), pp. 822–832.
[22] *cf.* House of Commons Home Affairs Committee, *Organised Crime* (Third Report, Session 1994–95), para. 8, for a fuller and slightly different definition.
[23] All quotations from the press release of August 8, 2001, "Organised Crime Poses a Major Threat to the UK": see www.ncis.co.uk/press.html.
[24] Press release of November 1999, "NCIS hits back at opponents of Regulation of Investigatory Powers Bill": see www.ncis.co.uk/press.html.
[25] Rather curiously, the press release denies that law enforcement powers are being extended, saying that the Act merely "updates law enforcement capability".
[26] Pradel, *op. cit.*, and n.9.
[27] House of Commons (above, n. 22), para. 55.
[28] *McIntosh v. H.M. Advocate* [2001] 3 W.L.R. 107, para. 4.
[29] arret du 8 avril, 1999 (decision of April 8, 1999).
[30] [1988] 2 S.C.R. 495.
[31] [1990] 1 S.C.R. 30.
[32] [1995] 2 S.C.R. 297.
[33] Above, p. 98.
[34] M. Delmas-Marty, *Corpus Iuris* (1997), p.1.
[35] G. Staple, "Serious and Complex Fraud—a New Perspective" (1993) 56 M.L.R. 127, p. 132; for similar sentiments, see J. Wood, "The Serious Fraud Office" [1989] Crim.L.R. 175, esp. p. 181.
[36] In *Saunders v. U.K.* (1997) 23 E.H.R.R. 313, discussed above, p. 58–60.
[37] Among the leading decisions are *Klass v. Germany* (1978) 2 E.H.R.R. 214 and *Malone v. U.K.* (1984) 7 E.H.R.R. 14.

[38] The *Volkszahlungsurteil* decision of 1983.

[39] This resembles the Canadian system, referred to and approved by the Strasbourg Court in *Chahal v. U.K.* (1996) 23 E.H.R.R. 413.

[40] Law of July 28, 2000.

[41] There is a provision allowing police informants to change their identity, which effectively makes it impossible for the defence to trace their antecedents. The provision was intended for use in trials connected with Mafia activities: law 119/1993, *Disciplina del cambiamento della generalita per la protezione di coloro che collaborano con la giustitia..*

[42] It should be recalled that, in the landmark decision in *Doorson v. Netherlands* (1996) 22 E.H.R.R. 330, the European Court of Human Rights emphasised that it is not sufficient for the court or prosecution to rely on the proposition that witnesses are frequently threatened in cases involving criminal organisations; it is necessary to demonstrate the existence of specific threats or reasonable grounds for a particular fear. See further lecture 2, pp. 77–80.

[43] See now the new version of article 500 of the *Codice di Procedura Penale*, introduced by law 63/2001.

[44] For analysis, see C. Gearty, "Terrorism and human rights: a case study in impending legal realities" (1999) 19 L.S. 367, at p. 371; H. Fenwick, *Civil Rights* (Longman, 2000), pp. 76–80.

[45] Home Office and Northern Ireland Office, *Legislation against Terrorism: a Consultation Paper* (1998), Chap. 3.

[46] *ibid.*, para. 3.12.

[47] These points were all pursued during debates on the Anti-Terrorism, Crime and Security Bill 2001, and led to the making of various concessions by the Government before it became an Act.

[48] The Austrian law is discussed at pp. 115–116 below.

[49] *cf.* the decision of the Strasbourg Court in *Chahal v. U.K.* (1996) 23 E.H.R.R. 413, and the recommendation of JUSTICE, *Under Surveillance* (1998), pp. 25–27.

[50] Pt 4 of the Act, especially ss. 25–26.

[51] Council of Europe, Recommendation No. R (96) 8.

[52] Joint Committee on Human Rights, Fifth Report, *Anti-Terrorism, Crime and Security Bill: Further Report* (HC 420, 2001).

[53] See the authorities discussed in lecture 2, pp. 56–61.

[54] See the decision on the right to trial within a reasonable time, in *Attorney-General's Reference No. 2 of 2001* [2002] Crim.L.R. 300, discussed above, p. 67.

[55] See the decision on the privilege against self-incrimination in *Brown v. Stott* [2001] 2 W.L.R. 817, discussed above, pp. 64–67.

[56] A. Ashworth, "Is the Criminal Law a Lost Cause?" (2000) 116 L.Q.R. 225.

[57] A thoughtful contribution is that of A. von Hirsch and N. Jareborg, "Gauging Criminal Harm: a Living Standard Analysis" (1991) 11 Oxford J.L.S. 1.

[58] See further Ashworth, *Sentencing and Criminal Justice* (3rd ed., Butterworths, 2000), Chap. 4.

[59] This is controversial, since there are some who argue that preventive goals should determine the focus of the criminal law: if a form of wrongdoing can be prevented by non-criminal sanctions of some kind then, even though it is more serious than some forms of wrongdoing which are the subject of criminal investigation and conviction, we should prefer the civil-regulatory approach. For John Braithwaite's arguments in this direction, and my counter-arguments, see A. Ashworth, "Is the Criminal Law a Lost Cause?" (2000) 116 L.Q.R. at 245–251.

[60] See *ibid.*, pp. 251–256, for further developments of these arguments.

[61] *S v. Coetzee and others* 1997 (3) SA 527, para. 220.

[62] G. Williams, *The Proof of Guilt* (3rd ed., Stevens, 1963), pp. 186–189; *cf.* A. Volokh, "*n* Guilty Men" (1997) 146 U.Pa.L.R. 173.

[63] R.A. Duff, *Trials and Punishments* (1986), p. 105.

[64] The rare case would be when an individual was acquitted through the operation of a human rights safeguard and there was a significant probability of dangerous conduct, which materialised. See lecture 2, pp. 77–80.

[65] See, *e.g.* P. Mirfield, *Silence, Confessions and Improperly Obtained Evidence* (Oxford U.P., 1997), pp. 23–28.

[66] For recent results, see A. Clancy, M. Hough, R. Aust and C. Kershaw, *Crime, Policing and Justice: the Experience of Ethnic Minorities—Findings from the 2000 British Crime Survey* (Home Office Research Study 223, 2001), Chap. 6.

[67] *cf.* Jack Straw, then Home Secretary, in an address to a Civil Service College Seminar, December 9, 1999: "Nor does it matter, I'm afraid, if the institution is in fact much fairer than the perception says. Perception often is reality when you're talking about confidence."

[68] An analogy might be drawn here with the recent determination of the House of Lords to insist that strict criminal liability has no place where an offence has a maximum penalty as high as 10 years' imprisonment: see *B v. DPP* [2000] 2 Cr.App.R. 65, *per* Lord Nicholls p. 73; *R. v. K.* [2001] 3 All E.R. 897, *per* Lord Bingham para. 23.

[69] Police and Criminal Evidence Act 1984, s.24.

[70] *ibid.*, s. 116.

[71] *ibid.*, s. 8.

[72] Regulation of Investigatory Powers Act 2000, s. 5(3); *cf.* s.28 of the same Act, where the directed surveillance of a person may be authorised if it is necessary "for the purpose of preventing or detecting crime"—as the interception of communications is more intrusive, the process of authorisation is more demanding.

[73] JUSTICE, *Under Surveillance* (1998); H. Fenwick, *Civil Rights* (2000).

[74] J. Pradel, "The Criminal Justice Systems facing the Challenge of Organized Crime" (1999) 69 *Revue Internationale de Droit Penal* 673.

[75] It should be noted that U.S. constitutional law has also been held to require judicial authorisation and supervision of intrusive surveillance: see *Berger v. New York* (1967) 388 U.S. 41, and Title III of the Omnibus Crime Control and Safe Streets Act 1968, followed by much state legislation, discussed in M.L. Miller and R.F. Wright, *Criminal Procedures* (Aspen, 1998), pp. 466–513.

[76] [2001] 2 W.L.R. 817, discussed at pp. 64–67 above.

[77] *Allen* [2001] UKHL 45.

[78] See the discussion of Dworkin's approach in Chapter 2D (iii) above.

[79] On the facts of *Brown v. Stott* this must be a contestable point; the penalty was a fine, penalty points and possibly disqualification from driving, and there are Strasbourg decisions (set out in Chap. 2B above) suggesting that this is sufficient compulsion to destroy the essence of the privilege against self-incrimination.

[80] (1988) 13 E.H.R.R. 379.

[81] S. Sedley, "Wringing Out the Fault: Self-Incrimination in the 21st Century", (2001) 52 N.I.L.Q. 107, p. 125.

[82] *Saunders v. U.K.* (1997) 23 E.H.R.R. 313, para. 74; see also *Teixeira de Castro v. Portugal* (1999) 28 E.H.R.R. 101, para. 36.

[83] *cf. Ozturk v. Turkey* (1984) 6 E.H.R.R. 409, and the thoughtful comments of Potter L.J. in *Han and Yau v. Customs and Excise Commissioners* [2001] EWCA Civ. 1048, para. 68.

[84] See n. 68 above.

[85] See the many decisions discussed in Emmerson and Ashworth, Chap. 4.

[86] See, *e.g.* Mr Straw's speech on the third reading: H.C. Deb., vol. 317, col. 1358.

[87] In a foreword to *Conventional Behaviour: Questions about the Human Rights Act, an Introduction for Public Authorities* (Home Office, 1999), quoted in F. Klug, *Values for a Godless Age* (Penguin, 2000), p. 27.

[88] Lord Irvine, "The Development of Human Rights in Britain under an Incorporated Convention on Human Rights", [1998] *Public Law* 221, p. 236.

[89] J. Straw, address to Civil Service College Seminar, December 9, 1999, p.1.

[90] *cf.* F. Klug, *Values for a Godless Age* (2000), esp. p. 197.

[91] T. Campbell, "Human Rights: a Culture of Controversy" (1999) 26 J.L.S. 6, p. 26.

[92] H.C. Deb., vol. 317, cols 1358–1359.

[93] See above, pp. 81–82.

[94] J. Straw, address to Civil Service College Seminar, December 9, 1999, p.5.

[95] (1996) 22 E.H.R.R. 330, discussed above, pp. 77–80.

[96] "The ECHR is nearly unique among human rights instruments. Because it balances and accompanies nearly everything it says about individual rights. Balances it with detailed statements of the limitations that can be placed on those rights." Straw (above, n. 89), p. 5; see also his speech of October 2, 2000, p.4. Apart from the example Mr Straw gave, relating to the *Doorson* decision on clashes between Art. 6 and Arts 3, 5 and 8, it is quite unclear what application this reasoning has to rights in Arts 5 and 6, as compared with rights in Arts 8–11 (to which his language more closely approximates). For the approach of the British judges, see above, pp. 64–68.

[97] In 1999 the United Nations issued a "Declaration on the Rights and Responsibilities of Individuals, Groups and Organs of Society to Promote and Protect Universally Recognised Human Rights and Fundamental Freedoms". Art. 18.1 comes closest to the wider notion of responsibilities espoused by Mr Straw: "Everyone has duties towards and within the community, in which alone the free and full development of his or her personality is possible." Clearly every individual has the duty to respect the rights of other individuals; but, apart from that, the only duties expressed in the remainder of the Convention are those of the State to promote and protect rights.

[98] D. Selbourne, *The Principle of Duty* (Abacus, 1997).

[99] A. Etzioni, *The Spirit of the Community: Rights, Responsibilities and the Communitarian Agenda* (Fontana, 1995), esp. part 2.

[100] For discussion, see D.A. Bell, *East meets West* (Princeton U.P., 2000) and A.J. Langlois, *The Politics of Justice and Human Rights: Southeast Asia and Universalist Theory* (Cambridge, 2001).

[101] Chan Sek Keong, "Rethinking the Criminal Justice System of Singapore for the 21st Century" (1999, unpublished), para. 19.

[102] *ibid.*, paras 9–11.

[103] *ibid.*, para. 48.

[104] For analysis of the practical prospects of the E.U. Charter, see, *e.g.*, K. Lenaerts, "Fundamental Rights in the European Union" (2000) 25 E.L.Rev. 575; F. Jacobs, "Human Rights in the European Union: the Role of the Court of Justice" (2001) 26 E.L.Rev. 331.

[105] H.L. Deb., vol. 582, col. 1272.

[106] M. Feeley and J. Simon, "Actuarial Justice: the Emerging New Criminal Law", in D. Nelken (ed.), *The Futures of Criminology* (Sage, 1994), p. 174.

[107] *ibid.*, p. 194; and see now T. Hope and R. Sparks (eds), *Crime, Risk and Insecurity* (Routledge, 2001).

[108] Notably R. Hood and S. Shute, *The Parole System at Work* (Home Office Research Study 202, 2000).

[109] For pioneering work on this which still repays study, see A.E. Bottoms, "Reflections on the Renaissance of Dangerousness" (1977) XVI *Howard Journal* 70.

[110] Home Office, Review of the Sentencing Framework got England and Wales, *Making Punishments Work* (2001), esp. para. 1.68; *cf.* A. Ashworth, *Sentencing and Criminal Justice* (3rd ed., 2000), Chap. 6, see the critical articles on the

Halliday Report by J. Roberts and by A. von Hirsch in (2002) *Punishment and Society*.

[111] D. Garland, *The Culture of Control* (2001), p. 132; see also C. Shearing, "Punishment and the Changing Face of Governance", (2001) *Punishment and Society* 203, and P.O'Malley (ed.), *Crime and the Risk Society* (1998).

[112] A. von Hirsch, "Law and Order", in A. von Hirsch and A. Ashworth (eds), *Principled Sentencing* (2nd ed., Hart, 1998), p. 413.

[113] M. Koskenniemi, "The Effect of Rights on Political Culture", in P. Alston (ed.), *The EU and Human Rights* (Oxford U.P., 1999), p. 100.

[114] See www.parliament.uk/commons/selcom/hrhome.htm.

[115] *e.g.* in *John Murray v. U.K.* (1996) 22 E.H.R.R. 29, and in *Saunders v. U.K.* (1997) 23 E.H.R.R. 313.

[116] See the discussion of *Brown v. Stott* and of *Allen* in Chap. 2, pp. 64–67, and above, p. 116–117; although I have argued that the reasoning of the Privy Council and House of Lords in these two cases is not faithful either to the Human Rights Act or to the Convention, there remains the possibility that the Strasbourg Court will treat the Convention as a "living instrument" and will carve out a new exception to reflect the fact that many Contracting States have legislation similar to the British. See Sedley (above, n. 81) for the argument that the Strasbourg Court ought to take this approach.

[117] Discussed above, pp. 77–80.

[118] *Doorson v. Netherlands* (1996) 22 E.H.R.R. 330, para. 72; see also *Van Mechelen v. Netherlands* (1997).

[119] (2000) 30 E.H.R.R. 1.

[120] *ibid.*, para. 61.

[121] *cf.* the decisions in *Jasper v. U.K.* (2000) 30 E.H.R.R. 441 and *Fitt v. U.K.* (2000) 30 E.H.R.R. 480, in both of which the Court divided almost equally on the adequacy of counterbalancing procedures.

[122] C. Douzinas, "Justice and Human Rights in Postmodernity", in C. Gearty and A. Tomkins (eds), *Understanding Human Rights* (Pinter, 1996), pp. 129–130, discussed in Chap. 2, above, pp. 86–87.

[123] This adapts the theory of J. Braithwaite and P. Pettit, *Not Just Deserts: a Republican Theory of Criminal Justice* (Oxford U.P., 1990); for criticism, see A. von Hirsch and A. Ashworth, "Not Not Just Deserts: a Response to Braithwaite and Pettit", (1992) 12 O.J.L.S. 83.

[124] See also A. Sanders and R. Young, *Criminal Justice* (2nd ed., Butterworths, 2000), who argue (p. 52) that when human rights and other interests are being compared, the approach "that is likely to enhance freedom the most" should be chosen, since the various conflicting considerations (human rights, protecting the innocent, convicting the guilty, protecting victims, maintaining public order, etc.) should be seen "as means to achieving the overriding goal of freedom."

[125] Above, n. 91 and text thereat.

[126] K. Günther, "The Legacies of Injustice and Fear: a European Approach to Human Rights and their Effects on Political Culture", in P. Alston (ed.), *The EU and Human Rights* (Oxford U.P., 1999); M. Loughlin, "Rights, Democracy and Law", in T. Campbell, K.D. Ewing and A. Tomkins (eds), *Sceptical Essays on Human Rights* (Oxford U.P., 2001).

[127] See, *e.g.* *Rowe and Davis* and *Doorson*, notes 117–118 above.

[128] See Emmerson and Ashworth, *Human Rights and Criminal Justice* (Sweet & Maxwell, 2001), Chap. 16.

INDEX

Index